A New Owner's
Guide to
SHAR-PEI

JG-112

Overleaf: Adult and puppy Shar-Pei owned by Dennis Kirby and Deanna Brown.

Opposite page: Adult Shar-Pei owned by Nancy Heller.

The Publisher wishes to acknowledge the following owners of the dogs in this book: Peter Belmont Jr., Laurel and Betty Colgate, Marylen Daly, Larry and Loraine Dawson, Ron and Barbara Dion, Dorie Fernandes, Bunny Franz, Sam and Kim Goza, Walter and Nancy Heller, Vicki L. Hester, Karen Kleinhans, Pastor Alan Klessig, Zella Llewellyn, Sherry L. Munsell, Elly Paulus, Bruce Lee Resnick, Mary Kaye Robison, Show Me Shar-Pei Kennels, Connie Tarrier, Thornton Photography, Doll Weil, and Laura Wiegand.

Photographers: Paulette Braun, B. Dion, Isabelle Francais, John Gillispie, Gravemann Photography, Robert Pearcy, Vincent Serbin, and Karen Taylor.

The author acknowledges the contribution of Judy Iby to the following chapters: Keeping Your Shar-Pei Healthy, Sport of Purebred Dogs, Identification and Finding the Lost Dog, Traveling with Your Dog, and Behavior and Canine Communication.

Distributed in the UNITED STATES to the Pet Trade by T.F.H. Publications, Inc., One T.F.H. Plaza, Neptune City, NJ 07753; distributed in the UNITED STATES to the Bookstore and Library Trade by National Book Network, Inc. 4720 Boston Way, Lanham MD 20706; in CANADA to the Pet Trade by H & L Pet Supplies Inc., 27 Kingston Crescent, Kitchener, Ontario N2B 2T6; Rolf C. Hagen Inc., 3225 Sartelon St. Laurent-Montreal Quebec H4R 1E8; in CANADA to the Book Trade by Vanwell Publishing Ltd., 1 Northrup Crescent, St. Catharines, Ontario L2M 6P5 ; in ENGLAND by T.F.H. Publications, PO Box 15, Waterlooville PO7 6BQ; in AUSTRALIA AND THE SOUTH PACIFIC by T.F.H. (Australia), Pty. Ltd., Box 149, Brookvale 2100 N.S.W., Australia; in NEW ZEALAND by Brooklands Aquarium Ltd. 5 McGiven Drive, New Plymouth, RD1 New Zealand; in Japan by T.F.H. Publications, Japan—Jiro Tsuda, 10-12-3 Ohjidai, Sakura, Chiba 285, Japan; in SOUTH AFRICA by Lopis (Pty) Ltd., P.O. Box 39127, Booysens, 2016, Johannesburg, South Africa. Published by T.F.H. Publications, Inc.
MANUFACTURED IN THE
UNITED STATES OF AMERICA
BY T.F.H. PUBLICATIONS, INC.

A New Owner's
Guide to
SHAR-PEI

Karen Kleinhans

Contents

Shar-Pei love to travel.

A trio of colorful Shar-Pei pups.

**The Shar-Pei became well established
due to the number of imports.**

PRODUCT OF CHINA

Nylabones® are safe chewing pacifiers for your Shar-Pei.

Wrinkles are limited to the face on the adult.

Shar-Pei puppies have cornered the market on cuteness.

HISTORY of the Chinese Shar-Pei

Without a doubt, the Chinese Shar-Pei is one of the most unique-looking breeds in the canine world. The animal's unusual appearance and adaptable, intelligent personality are among the many reasons for its amazing popularity. In the past few decades, we have seen the number of registered Chinese Shar-Pei grow from perhaps a dozen in 1977 to many thousands today.

Most people do not realize that Shar-Pei existed in the southern provinces of China during the Han Dynasty (206 BC-220 AD). It is generally believed that they originated in and around the village of Dah Let, in southern China's Kwongtung Province, near the South China Sea. This is apparent in the paintings and statuettes found in museums today. The blue-black tongue and other characteristics of the Shar-Pei point to the Chow-Chow as either an ancestor or at least as sharing a common ancestry with the Shar-Pei. It is known that both breeds existed in the same period and may be descended from the Tibetan Mastiff. This theory is substantiated by the Orthopedic Foundation for Animals' classification of the Shar-Pei as a giant breed because of the breed's rapid growth pattern, even though the Shar-Pei is a medium-sized breed. (The Tibetan Mastiff is a giant breed.)

The Chinese Shar-Pei has deeply seeded roots in the southern provinces of China that can be traced as far back as the Han Dynasty (200 A.D.).

Dogs were a practical part of Chinese peasant life; those not meeting the standards of intelligence and purpose were most likely used for food and clothing. A weak dog had no function in the Chinese home. Shar-Pei were undoubtedly selectively bred for intelligence, strength, and lordly scowl, which was thought to give a menacing appearance. The blue-black tongue, exposed when the dog barked, was thought to frighten off evil spirits. One early British author studying dogs in the Orient described the native dogs she found in China as being mixed with Mastiff, Chow, Bulldog, and street dog, and

as being developed in each area of the vast country to serve a different purpose.

As a result of their purpose, the dogs in southern China were athletic, short coated, and well muscled, with a good clean bite. The original Down Homes Kennel dogs fit this description, many of them being larger than the typical Shar-Pei today.

In central China, where farming and herding were predominant, the Shar-Pei developed a herding instinct and an almost terrier-type ratting instinct. The dogs were described as being of medium size, short coupled, with large bones and athletic style. Their legs were shorter than those in the south and their bulk was more compact than their relatives farther to the north. Today, we can still see certain "ratting" instincts. Many Shar-Pei will naturally go to ground for rodents, will attack squirrels, cats and small animals unless they have been raised with them, and will herd and head cattle and sheep if given a chance.

This Shar-Pei puppy is practicing his ancient herding instincts on an uncooperative Peahen!

(Many can be seen exercising this instinct in the home, herding the other dogs away from the food bowl!) They do not bark like herding dogs, nor do they dig and chew like terriers. It is possible that these characteristics are present in terriers and herding dogs, not because they are necessary, but because many of the dogs in those AKC groups came from the same European root stock, while the Shar-Pei has its root stock half a world away.

In the northern part of China, where small communities live through the long cold winters in remote villages, it is important that the dog be quiet and calm if it is to spend long hours in the same small space with many family members. Since extra dogs were used for food, the thicker-bodied, more

In the remote villages of northern China, the Shar-Pei had to adjust to small, cramped quarters. This little pup may be comfortable in a picnic basket, but shouldn't have to live there.

heavily muscled dogs were preferred as better meat sources. Chows spring from a similar background and both breeds probably share a recent common ancestry. Some Shar-Pei had longer coats, called "Song Ye" coats in China and "bear coats" in the US. They had heavier bones and were more placid in temperament than the other types of Chinese dogs.

In the Shar-Pei, we see the Chow line ancestry in the black tongue, the recessive "bear coat," entropion (a condition in which the eyelashes roll inward), the deep body style, etc. The Bulldog ancestry is seen in some short necks that are low set on the shoulders, some "bulldog fronts," thick bodies, and certain breathing and other genetic problems shared only by

The Shar-Pei's common ancestry with the Chow can easily be seen in the breed's black tongue.

Bulldogs and Shar-Pei. It is probably safe to assume that these two breeds were crossed into native stock—in the south for fighting and in the north for food (which was the original purpose of the Chow)—along with perhaps some Mastiff and other breeds as they came along with their British masters to the Far East.

Along the South China Sea, the area originally given credit for producing the Chinese Shar-Pei, is an area of cities where gambling is a favorite pastime. Considering that betting was already going on with cock fights and pitting other breeds of dogs against each other, it was inevitable that the Shar-Pei would eventually be used for fighting. This pastime was an outgrowth of the cultural love of wagering, particularly on the outcome of physical conflict. As a result of the Shar-Pei's usage in these contests, breeders further developed the bristly coat and loose skin to improve the breed's ability to win. "Shar-Pei" translates to "sandy dog" ("shar" meaning sand of gritty texture and "pei" meaning dog). The tiny ears and deep-set eyes were naturally protected by their size and shape. The extra wrinkling made it possible for a dog under attack to turn and defend itself more easily, and gave the dog's opponent a mouthful of prickly skin! However, the Shar-Pei lacked two vital traits of successful fighting dogs. Firstly, they were too small to be effective against the mastiff family of dogs. Secondly, their temperaments were not naturally aggressive to the degree required. They were drugged or given wine to cause aggression, but they were still not real competition for other breeds such as English Mastiffs and Bulldogs, which were soon introduced to China. Once these heavier dogs with fiercer temperaments were crossbred into the fighting stock, the Shar-Pei proved to be no match for the resulting dogs. No longer in demand, the Shar-Pei's breeding was neglected, resulting in a rapid decrease in numbers.

Although these Shar-Pei puppies are having fun wrestling with each other, the breed's non-aggressive temperament made it unsuccessful in dog fighting as a sport.

With the onset of Mao Tse-tung and Communist China, the breed was nearly destroyed. A heavy tax was levied so that only the wealthy could afford a dog as a companion. Dog breeding was banned completely and by 1950 there were few specimens of this noble dog left; the breed was about to be lost to the world.

Although a few Shar-Pei had been imported into the United States in the 1960s, a real interest in the breed did not develop until Matgo Law, a Hong Kong breeder, wrote his 1973 article in *Dogs Magazine*, appealing to American dog lovers to help save this dying breed. There were over 200 replies from anxious buyers, but, with limited numbers available, it was some time before the puppies came to the United States. While the rescue breeding was undertaken with very few specimens, necessitating inbreeding, it is fortunate that those early dogs were the products of "survival of the fittest" and therefore carried a strong, yet diverse, gene pool. (The dogs imported by Mr. Law carry the kennel name "Down Homes" and some had no pedigree information available. Almost all Shar-Pei pedigrees can be traced back to Down Homes Sweet Pea, Down Homes Anne Revival, Down Homes Kung Fu, Down Homes China Souel, Down Homes Mui Chu and a few other Down Homes dogs.) The fact that these dogs were probably all crossed with something else accounted for the variety in the breed, especially in the early years. Each area of China probably contributed dogs that were crossed with different breeds and to different degrees.

Shar-Pei imports from China to the United States soared after Matgo Law's famous appeal to American dog lovers to save the Shar-Pei from becoming an extinct breed.

Many of the early dogs had longer legs than what is popular today, with smaller heads and almost a complete outgrowth of wrinkling. These dogs

PRODUCT OF CHINA

Mi-Wei's Autumn Song Of Shea, a bear coat female, owned by Bunny Franz. In their early years, Shar-Pei were probably crossed with Chow Chow, which can account for this thicker coat. were athletic, typically good movers, with longer necks that were well placed high on the shoulders, and had a well balanced look. The West Coast breeders, in California and Texas particularly, kept this style of dog while a different look was being developed in the Midwest and East. (Today the regional differences are much more subtle as in other breeds.)

The pioneers of this breed in the United States had their work cut out for them. There were few Shar-Pei spread across the large country, with no definitive information available. A few of the pioneers were Ernest and Madeline Albright, Ho Wun Kennels; Mr. and Mrs. Victor Seas, Walnut Lanes Kennel; Lois Alexander, Siskiyou Kennels; and Walter "Dugan" Skinner, Shur-Du Kennels.

Until about 1984, there were certain generalizations that could be made about the dogs bearing different types of coats. Horse coats were said to be taller, lighter in bone, more agile, lighter in head, and more aggressive in temperament. Brush coats were said to be heavier in bone, carrying more wrinkling into adulthood, cobbier (a word used in much of the advertising of the time meaning short-bodied, compact), larger in head, and more placid in temperament. The differences were real and they were explained by the differences in the genetic roots of the original import dogs. These differences are much less evident today.

A problem with the public perception of the Chinese Shar-Pei is that most photos of the breed tend to be of puppies, usually between three and six months of age. They may have props with them, but they seldom have humans in the photos, or any other reference to size. The photos are usually close-ups to show the wrinkling. This often leads people to a mistaken idea of both the size and appearance of the adult dog.

The Shar-Pei is a puppy breed, unlike some other breeds that are awkward as puppies and not as attractive as the adults apart from the inherent "cuteness" of anything small and young. Breeds such as Pointers and Great Danes are awkward looking puppies, and it is likely to be over a year before they begin to come together. Other breeds, such as Poodles, Akitas, and Golden Retrievers, are cute from birth to adulthood. While the Shar-Pei emerges from puppy cuteness as it grows, those fans of the breed find the adult to be quite a handsome, striking dog. Wrinkling is usually limited in the full-size adult dog to facial wrinkles and four or five rolls on the shoulders. This may not bother the show breeder but is often lamented by the average owner or would-be owner.

The Chinese Shar-Pei Club of America (CSPCA) held its first meeting in Oregon in 1974, with its National Specialty

Wrinkling is usually limited to the face in the full-size adult. This is ZL-Rho-Z's Remmington Steel.

14

Although the Shar-Pei adult is not as handsome as some other breeds, Shar-Pei puppies have cornered the market on cuteness.

show held in Hinckley, Illinois in 1978. Although the club later split into two distinct organizations, it reunited in 1980 and is the parent club for this breed today and a member of the AKC.

In those early years, curiosity led to television shows and numerous print articles devoted to this fascinating breed, yet the breeders themselves were sailing in uncharted waters! But the devotion this breed inspires as well as its inherent loyalty and stoicism made the frustrations and setbacks easier to bear. By 1980, the Chinese Shar-Pei Club of America registry was able to close foreign registrations, limiting the importing significantly. Within ten years of the breed's arrival in the US, it was the most rapidly growing breed in the country (perhaps in the world) and 20 years later was entering the AKC, taking its rightful place in the canine world.

CHARACTERISTICS of the Shar-Pei

The first question a potential Shar-Pei owner will ask is, "What are they like?" While the answers are as varied as the dogs themselves, some things stand out above the others. The answers that immediately spring to the mind of those who have lived with these dogs are intelligent, funny, loyal, and easy to keep. Indeed, you may find it is hard to have just one! (And contrary to the nasty rumors that keep resurfacing, they do *not* get "mold in their folds!" The skin is loose, leaving the wrinkles very mobile, so they don't need any special care!)

The intelligence of this breed truly requires an owner at least as intelligent as the dog! Given a home where the owner is timid or does not pay close attention to the training of the dog, the dog could definitely take charge or become neurotic, depending on the environment. This breed is incredibly respectful of the leader of the pack and it is the human owners who must hold that position. All new owners are encouraged to attend a training class and learn about the manner in which dogs think and perceive things. You will find that once you learn how to teach your Shar-Pei what is expected and what is unacceptable, you will have the finest in canine companionship. And like most dogs left to make their own decisions in a complex human world, some will become dominating or aggressive, while others will become fearful or shy. It is truly best, as is with any breed, to have a socialized,

Once your Shar-Pei learns what is expected and what is unacceptable, you will have the finest in canine companionship, and there is no better house pet.

16

obedience-trained Shar-Pei. The dog will be happier, and you will be too.

Shar-Pei are extremely adaptable to all types of homes, doing equally well in apartments or on farms; with single owners or with families with small children; fully crate-trained with either limited house freedom or the run of the whole house. They are *not* "outside" dogs, as they can not handle winter and summer in the backyard with a dog

A puppy's personality and temperament begin to develop through socialization with the dam and littermates.

house. Most dogs have an undercoat that acts as an insulation against cold and heat. Shar-Pei do not have this protective undercoat and are much more susceptible to

Shar-Pei are extremely adaptable to all types of homes and lifestyles. Small children and Shar-Pei quickly become friends for life!

extremes in the weather. Please enjoy your Shar-Pei in a protected environment.

They are medium-sized, compact dogs, which means that they are not too large to fit easily in most apartments. Most will top out in height just beneath an adult person's knee. The sturdy build of a Shar-Pei holds up well against toddlers' antics, and these dogs' natural patience with the young make them an excellent choice for a family with children. Their inherently protective nature has led many families to extol the virtues of Shar-Pei as their family companion (and to get a second and third Shar-Pei as a member of the family).

The Shar-Pei's natural patience with the young makes it a perfect choice for a home with small children.

While their primary role in today's society is that of a pet and companion, they are also adept as family guard dogs. They bark to warn that someone is nearby, but once the okay is given by the owner, most are likely to bowl over the newcomer with affection. Many a time Shar-Pei have thwarted an intruder with simply their deep, powerful bark and their scowling face! Outside their own environment, they tend to be a bit reserved and watchful, not easily startled, but not the type to go with strangers very willingly.

In your home, they will quickly adapt to the schedule you set. I encourage all new owners to crate-train their pets. Even if you will eventually allow your dog unlimited access to your home, it is nice to be able to keep your pet quietly out of the way sometimes. Perhaps you have a workman at the house and

you don't want the dog underfoot, or maybe you are hosting a party of some kind and anticipate having guests who may not have the same fondness for pets that you

All new owners are advised to crate-train their Shar-Pei, even if it will eventually be given free roam of the house. Crates simplify training and housebreaking.

have. You can simply put your Shar-Pei in his "bedroom" (his crate), and if he is trained that this is a positive, safe place for him to stay, he will not resent the crate but will view it as his own personal space.

Shar-Pei are not an overly active breed, unless this is your typical lifestyle. While they can be very playful, good jogging companions or obedience competitors, they are also excellent quiet time companions. They are content to lay at your feet, require an energy outlet equal to a nice walk once a day (or some play time in a safe, fenced yard), and enjoy occasional displays of affection. Again, this area of your Shar-Pei's life will be determined by how you live. This is not a breed that becomes destructive without major exercise time each day, nor is it a breed that constantly needs cuddling for security. Shar-Pei are independent in nature but enjoy sharing their lives with humans.

Your Shar-Pei will live its life the way you do; it will happily go for a walk with you, lay content at your feet, and appreciate all displays of affection.

They tend to be "whole family" dogs in that they do not choose just one family member to bond with. Using their intelligence, they quickly learn each family member's likes and dislikes. Your Shar-Pei may sleep on one family member's bed, yet stay out of a bedroom where it has never been invited. He may play rough and tumble with the man of the house, but rest quietly at the feet of the elderly grandparent.

Shar-Pei seem to have a sense of humor, and once they find what makes the owner laugh and smile, you can count on them to continue to perform! They are very in tune with the moods of the household and respond accordingly. Like most dogs, they see their prime objectives as making the owner happy and safe, fitting in, and watching out for the other members of the family "pack."

Once your Shar-Pei learns what pleases you and makes you laugh, you can count on him to perform!

In play, they often use their front feet much like a cat, batting at their playmate. In play with humans, they often take the human's arm in their mouth as a gentle sign of affection. Perhaps the most dominant physical motion in play with other dogs is the "hip check" where they swing their bodies around and use their hip to bump their playmate out of the way!

A very strong breed characteristic is their dislike of water, even rain! Many are the adult, well-trained, stable, and strong Shar-Pei that are reduced to a heap of unhappiness at the sight of rain when they go outside to take care of business! Some enjoy rivers and lakes, but few have taken a liking to the family pool. Bathing is a necessity that is best taught early, before they are big enough to challenge you in a slippery wet tub!

With their short coats, groomers refer to them as "wash and wear" dogs. No extensive bathing or grooming requirements are necessary for your companion. Bathe your Shar-Pei occasionally, trim his nails and clean his ears—add some training and love and it is a recipe for happiness like none other!

STANDARD for the Shar-Pei

P lease note: The roman portions of this chapter are the standard, and the italicized portions are the explanations or clarifications. While the official standard is used for judging purposes, the other points in this section are added to give you a more detailed explanation of the standard.

Oftentimes, a great pet is perfect in all ways, except that it is lacking (or has too much of) something. It may be too tall or too short, or possess any number of traits that the breeder doesn't want used for breeding or showing. This does not mean the dog is unhealthy or even inferior. It just may not fit what the breeder's idea of perfection is. On the other hand, if you are looking for a show or breeding dog, purchasing a Shar-Pei with no major or disqualifying faults is preferred.

Although there is no such thing as a perfect Shar-Pei, choosing a puppy with no major or disqualifying faults puts you well on your way to a great show or breeding dog.

GENERAL APPEARANCE

An alert, dignified, active, compact dog of medium size and substance, square in profile, close-coupled, the well proportioned head slightly but not overly large for the body. The short, harsh coat, the loose skin covering the head and body, the small ears, the "hippopotamus" muzzle shape and the high set tail impart to the Shar-Pei a look peculiar to him alone. The loose skin and wrinkles covering the head, neck and body are superabundant in puppies but these features may be limited to the head, neck and withers in the adult.

SIZE, PROPORTION, SUBSTANCE

The preferred height is 18 to 20 inches at the withers. The preferred weight is 40 to 55 pounds. The dog is usually larger and more square bodied than the bitch but both appear well proportioned.

Proportion—The height of the Shar-Pei from the ground to

the withers is approximately equal to the length from the point of breastbone to the point of rump.

This is why you will hear the words "square" and "cobby" used to describe this breed.

HEAD

Large, slightly but not overly, proudly carried and covered with profuse wrinkles on the forehead continuing into side wrinkles framing the face.

Eyes—Dark, small, almond-shaped and sunken, displaying a scowling expression. In the dilute colored dogs the eyes may be lighter.

This deep-set eye with profuse wrinkling about the head should still be clear and easily seen. Also, one finds that the Shar-Pei has limited peripheral vision. As a medium-sized dog, the Shar-Pei may perceive a person moving unexpectedly from the side or above as a threatening figure. With this in mind, a stranger would be less likely to startle a Shar-Pei by approaching the dog from the front, perhaps by bending down.

Ears: Extremely small rather thick, equilateral triangles in shape, slightly rounded at the tips, edges of the ears may curl. Ears lie flat against the head, are set wide apart and forward on the skull, pointing toward the eyes. The ears have the ability to move. Pricked ears are a disqualification.

Many times breeders are questioned about the small, triangular ear of this breed. These oddly shaped ears are a natural, uncropped triangle. Many times they are curled or wrinkled like the rest of the head. The ears do have erectile power, and the Shar-Pei can move the ear, however, an ear carried as a prick ear is a disqualification.

Skull: Flat and broad, the stop moderately defined.

Muzzle: One of the distinctive features of the breed. It is broad and full with no suggestion of snipiness. (The length from nose to stop is approximately the same as from stop to occiput.) Nose—Large and wide and darkly pigmented, preferably black but any color nose conforming to the general coat color of the dog is acceptable. In dilute colors, the preferred nose is self-colored. Darkly pigmented cream Shar-Pei may have some light pigment either in the center of their noses or on their entire nose. The lips and top of the muzzle are well padded and may cause a slight bulge at the base of the nose.

Seen from the front, the head of a Chinese Shar-Pei may remind you of a hippopotamus. There are still many different head types in Shar-Pei, from the "meat mouth" which is heavily padded, to the "bone mouth" which is less fleshy. Either type, and those in between, is acceptable. Many breeders refer to the smaller-headed dogs as being more "Chinese" because the larger heads are a result of the breeding done in the USA.

TONGUE, ROOF OF MOUTH, GUMS AND FLEWS

Solid bluish-black is preferred in all coat colors except in dilute colors, which have a solid lavender pigmentation. A spotted tongue is a major fault. A solid pink tongue is a disqualification. (Tongue colors may lighten due to heat stress; care must be taken not to

A solid bluish-black tongue is preferred in all coat colors except in dilute colors, which should have a solid lavender tongue.

confuse dilute pigmentation with a pink tongue.)

One of the distinctive features of the breed is a solid, bluish-black tongue and mouth (lavender in dilutes). When trying to pick a show dog, it is important to note that the tongue color will lighten as the dog exercises and warms up (or in warm summer temperatures). Shar-Pei are usually born with solid pink tongues and the black or lavender pigmentation comes as the puppy ages. Most puppies have solid pigment on their tongues by six to eight weeks of age. You may find a pup that is show quality in all ways except for the tongue pigment and that is why the breeder is selling the puppy as a pet, to be neutered. This could be a great way to get a companion that has all the outward looks of a great show dog! At this time, it is also noteworthy to point out that, like other short muzzled breeds, the Shar-Pei is potentially heat susceptible.

Teeth: Strong, meeting in a scissors bite. Deviation from a scissors bite is a major fault.

NECK, TOPLINE, BODY

Neck: Medium length, full and set well into the shoulders. There are moderate to heavy folds of loose skin and abundant dewlap about the neck and throat.

Topline: The topline dips slightly behind the withers, slightly rising over the short, broad loin. Chest—Broad and deep with the brisket extending to the elbow and rising slightly under the loin. Back—Short and close-coupled.

Ch. Tai-Pan's Odie of Kasu, CD TT ROM, "alert, regal and dignified" as the standard requires, and certified for hips and eyes.

Croup: Flat, with the base of the tail set extremely high, clearly exposing an uptilted anus. Tail–The high set tail is a characteristic feature of the Shar-Pei. The tail is thick and round at the base, tapering to a fine point and curling over or to either side of the back. The absence of a complete tail is a disqualification.

Note the moderate folds of loose skin on the neck and throat of this brush coat Shar-Pei.

FOREQUARTERS

Shoulder: Muscular, well laid back and sloping.

Forelegs: When viewed from the front, straight, moderately spaced, with elbows close to the body. When viewed from the side, the forelegs are straight, the pasterns are strong and flexible. The bone is substantial but never heavy and is of moderate length. Removal of front dewclaws is optional.

Feet: Moderate in size, compact and firmly set, not splayed.

HINDQUARTERS

Muscular, strong, and moderately angulated. The metatarsi (hocks) are short, perpendicular to the ground and parallel to each other when viewed from the rear. Hind dewclaws must be removed. Feet as in front.

COAT

The extremely harsh coat is one of the distinguishing features of the breed. The coat is absolutely straight and offstanding on the main trunk of the body but generally lies somewhat flatter on the limbs. The coat appears healthy without being shiny or lustrous. Acceptable coat lengths may range from the extremely short "horse coat" up to the "brush coat," not to exceed one inch in length at the withers. A soft coat, a wavy coat, a coat in excess of one inch in length at the withers or a coat that has been trimmed is a major fault. The Shar-Pei is shown in its natural state.

Color

Only solid colors are acceptable. A solid colored dog may have shading, primarily darker down the back and on the ears. The shading must be variations of the same body color (except in sables) and may include darker hairs throughout the coat. The following colors are a disqualifying fault: Not a solid color, i.e., Albino; Brindle; Parti-colored (patches); Spotted (including spots, ticked or roaning); Tan-Pointed pattern (including typical black and tan or saddled patterns).

Only solid colors are acceptable in the Shar-Pei. This sable-colored bitch is seen here with three of her pups, two black and one cream.

In relation to the standard of the breed, no one solid color is preferred to any other solid color. The following are the descriptions of coat colors that were used by the Registrar of the Chinese Shar-Pei Club of America prior to the breed's acceptance by AKC. They are included here so that you may familiarize yourself with acceptable solid colors.

__Group A: Basic Colors.__ Has black (charcoal) pigmentation, i.e., skin, nose, tongue, mouth/flews and footpads. Nails may be lighter.

Cream: An "off-white" color. May have darker ears and shading along the dorsal line. May be described as light cream, cream or dark cream.

Fawn: A very light tan/golden color ranging to a dark tan/ golden. Some fawns with dark fawn coats have a pronounced red tinge. May have darker shading along the dorsal line. Red fawns may have lighter colored skin, eyes and toenails. They should have a solid colored nose and foot pads. May be described as light fawn, fawn, dark fawn, or red fawn.

Red: Mahogany to rich chestnut (example: Irish Setter). The coat color is uniform over the body, neck, head and legs. Very little variation.

Brown: A medium to dark brown color. The coat color is uniform over the body, neck, head and legs. Very little variation.

Sable: A lacing of black hairs over a lighter ground color. The coat color is uniform over the body, neck, head and legs. Little variation.

28

Silver: Includes blue, grey and taupe. A bluish/silverish smoky color. The coat color is uniform over the body, neck and legs. Little variation.

Black: True black. May have a blue, grey, brown or red tinge on the sides. The coat color is uniform over the body, neck, head and legs. Very little variation.

Group B: Dilute Colors. *No black (charcoal) pigmentation anywhere on dog. Skin, nose and nails are self colored blending with the coat color. Eyes may be light or dark. Tongues may vary light to dark lavender.*

Cream dilute: An "off-white" color. May have darker shading on the ears and along the dorsal line.

Apricot dilute: Similar but lighter in color than the five-point-red dilute. A distinct apricot color ranging in shades from light to dark.

Only the apricot puppy in this trio of Shar-Pei is a dilute. The other two are a cream and a blue.

Five-point-red dilute: A distinct deep red fawn varying to dark red color. Coat color is uniform over the dog. Little variation. The five points are: nose, eyes, skin, footpads and anus.

Chocolate dilute: A medium to dark color (example: milk or dark chocolate). The coat color is uniform over the dog. Little variation. Includes liver.

Sable dilute: A lacing of dark colored hairs over a lighter ground color. The coat color is uniform.

Silver dilute: Includes blue, grey and taupe. A bluish/silver smoky color. Coat color is uniform over the dog. Little variation. Nose is slate. Mouth/tongue is lavender. Skin, eyes, footpads and nails are self-colored.

Chinese Shar-Pei and Foo Dogs come in any color. This is Ruffles Red Tsunami Benchmark, an apricot dilute. A dilute has no black pigmentation anywhere, and Shar-Pei never come in green!

Group C: Not a Solid Color (a disqualification).

Albino, Brindle (with a typical tiger stripe pattern), Parti-colored (patches of two or more colors), Spotted (spots, ticked, roaning), Tan-pointed patterns (like German

Shepherds or Doberman Pinschers). Please remember these last five are disqualifications.

GAIT

The movement of the Shar-Pei is to be judged at a trot. The gait is free and balanced with the feet tending to converge on a center line of gravity when the dog moves at a vigorous trot. The gait combines good forward reach and a strong drive in the hindquarters. Proper movement is essential.

Like most sound moving breeds, Shar-Pei tend to single track when moving at a brisk trot. The rear feet will converge more quickly than the front, but in any event, the movement should be clean coming and going with good reach and drive from the side. Please note the strength of the wording in the standard: proper movement is essential.

TEMPERAMENT

Regal, alert, intelligent, dignified, lordly, scowling, sober and snobbish, essentially independent and somewhat standoffish with strangers, but extreme in his devotion to his family. The Shar-Pei stands firmly on the ground with a calm, confident stature.

The Shar-Pei is a proud breed, presenting to the public the image of strength and power, but in the home they are devoted and humorous companions.

MAJOR FAULTS
1. Deviation from a Scissors Bite.
2. Spotted Tongue.
3. A Soft Coat, a Wavy Coat, a coat in excess of one inch in length at the withers or a coat that has been trimmed.

DISQUALIFICATIONS
1. Pricked Ears.
2. Solid Pink Tongue.
3. Absence of a Complete Tail.
4. Not a Solid Color.

CONCLUSION

The standard of any breed defines the ideal example of that breed. The picture you get in your mind from reading this

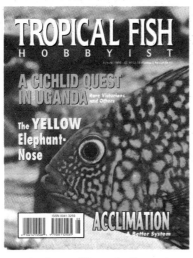

In order to learn the standard, one must first understand what each word means. Pinoak Brown Baggie's profile shows off his stop, *step up from muzzle to backskull.*

written standard is the picture of the ideal Shar-Pei. Regardless of the purpose of your choice of dog, knowing the standard helps you understand your individual dog's attributes and drawbacks. This is especially important if you plan to breed and/or show your dog. If you do plan to do either of these things, learn any of the words you don't immediately understand, like perhaps occiput or pastern. The more you learn about your breed, the more you know about your own dog, and this knowledge makes the difference between success and failure. Even if your Shar-Pei will be a simple life companion with no plans for a big show career or litters of pups, you can certainly enjoy learning about your dog's "family background!" And in all cases, the standard is a perfect place to start.

SELECTING the Right Shar-Pei

I f you have decided that the Shar-Pei may be the breed for you, the next step is to visit as many breeders as possible. You will learn more from these visits than any book could ever teach you! Because the choices are so numerous, you need to make some decisions ahead of the purchase date. These decisions can be made easier by the more Shar-Pei you see and the more breeders you talk to. Breeders can be found in your local newspaper, at dog shows, or by writing to the Chinese Shar-Pei Club of America.

SHOW DOG, BREEDING DOG, OR COMPANION PET

While for many breeders there is no difference between these three distinctions in their own personal kennels (my show dogs were also my companion pets!), it will make a difference in what they are willing to sell, and will be one of the first questions they will ask you. A show dog is an animal the breeder would like to see exhibited, and may even require that it be shown. It is an exemplary specimen of the breed, is sound and has a good show attitude, and has a promising show career. Many kennels have dogs that they consider "breeding dogs." These are typically dogs that could be show dogs, but perhaps the breeder doesn't require them to be shown, or perhaps they don't have the right attitude or top winning looks, despite their impressive pedigrees. These are the dogs

A breeder may categorize his stock as either show, breeding, or companion. It is important that you know what you are looking for in a Shar-Pei before you purchase one.

that small kennels start with and large kennels rely upon as their foundation for top show dogs. What is typically called a "pet" dog is simply a Shar-Pei that the breeder sees no sense in showing or breeding. Perhaps it has a flaw that the breeder does not wish to continue to produce, or perhaps it just isn't as eye catching as most show dogs.

These foundation dogs for ZL Shar-Pei came directly from China.

If you want a show dog, expect to pay a higher price. Like any sport, the best "equipment," and the finest "costumes" cost money. To produce a good show dog, the breeder has invested time, energy, and money, and could keep and show the dog

This is Show Me Kim Lous Ching Lynn, an eight-year-old female cream horse coat.

himself instead of selling it for a small sum. As a pet, a show quality dog is no different than a pet quality dog. The difference is that you would not be very likely to win a dog show with a pet quality dog (it has been known to happen, but rarely). If you do plan to show, make sure you do a tremendous amount of research, and work with a breeder you like and trust as this will give you your best chance at a successful and rewarding show career.

Let me make one warning at this point. If you think you can buy a nice show dog, have a few litters, and make some money, think again. Showing and breeding is an expensive hobby, and done properly, with the health and well-being of the dog in mind, is almost certainly *not* financially rewarding! Since most hobbies are not money making ventures, yet give lasting joy, don't think you have to mortgage your house to have some fun either!

If you want a dog you can breed, start by asking yourself "why?" If you want to improve the breed, to go to shows and learn, to invest in good stock and solid health care, and to enjoy the fun of raising wonderful, healthy babies, then start studying the breed and its breeders with that in mind. If you want a litter so that your children can experience birth, or because you think you can make a little extra money, stop right there. Puppies produced for the wrong reasons are the most likely to end up in sad situations, needing rescue or being euthanized in a shelter. Think carefully about your decision to breed dogs. Once you've concluded that you want to make a positive contribution to purebred dogs, and to the Shar-Pei in particular, then start studying. You will want to learn about pedigrees and breeders and have a strong working knowledge of the various bloodlines before you purchase your foundation Shar-Pei.

Perhaps you simply want a great companion or a loving dog to share your life with. Then a pet quality Shar-Pei could be the optimum choice for you! When breeders advertise "pet quality," they intend for that dog to be spayed or neutered, not bred and shown. Why? Well, it may not be the perfect example of a Shar-Pei—maybe it has a small flaw, like some pink on its tongue, or just does not have the "look" that is winning in the show ring. It does *not* mean that it is an inferior or unhealthy Shar-Pei. Pet quality Shar-Pei purchased from reputable breeders are as healthy, sound, intelligent and enjoyable as the show dogs—after all, its littermates or parents are top show dogs!

No matter what type of Shar-Pei you are looking for: pet, show, or breeding, you should do your homework, ask questions, and proceed with caution. Whether show, breeding, or pet quality, all are Shar-Pei and should exhibit Shar-Pei temperaments, be intelligent companions, and fill your life with enjoyment.

MALE OR FEMALE

Many people ask for females, but don't know why they have that preference. Some feel that females make better pets, or are less aggressive or dominant. In Shar-Pei, the males are no more strong

The sex and color of the puppy you choose is truly a matter of personal preference. Temperament is the key factor!

willed than the females. If you don't spay/neuter, you will face either heat cycles in the females or territory marking by the males. (Males do not mark their territory inside their home, but the bushes are fair game!) Indeed, there is little difference in temperament, cleanliness or companionship pleasure between the male or female. You may still have a preference, but now you know that either one will be great!

PUPPY OR ADULT

Puppies are so darn cute but those grown dogs are so well behaved! Most people want a puppy, regardless of their breed choice. The thing to remember about puppies is that the optimum age to get one is 8 to 16 weeks. If they are much younger, they have not learned all they should from their littermates and mother. The optimum bonding and learning time is between 8 and 16 weeks. This does not mean that an older pup will not learn, this is just the best timing if you are looking for a small pup.

If you don't have the time or energy to invest in housebreaking or basic training, an older pup or adult could be the choice for you. A well-adjusted adult that has been treated well makes an almost unnoticeable adjustment to a new home. A dog that has shared his life with a kennel full of other dogs may miss their companionship briefly, but soon learns that an only dog doesn't have to share any of the "good stuff!" If you are considering an older dog, breeders may have former show dogs that they are retiring, or know of a client who can no longer keep their adult. You can also check with local Shar-Pei clubs about their "rescue dogs." These are dogs whose owners abandoned them, left them at shelters, or abused them. The club-run rescue organizations are very thorough in researching and caring for their rescue dogs, which means that if that is the direction you go, you will get a great deal of support from the club in additon to a devoted and grateful companion.

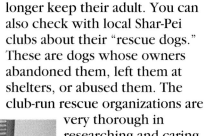

Small hobby breeders have the advantage of socializing puppies in their homes. These young Shar-Pei will have no problem adjusting to their new home.

SPAYING/NEUTERING

First, let me dispel any ideas you have that spaying or neutering your pet will make him lethargic, lazy, or any different at all. There are many reasons to encourage spaying and neutering. A spayed female does not have the mess of heat cycles, has no chance for accidental breeding, and has no chance of any disease of her reproductive organs. A neutered male will not produce unwanted pups, will feel less territorial and therefore less likely to mark every bush he sees, and will be safe from testicular diseases. Many breeders sell their dogs

Good breeders care about the well-being of the dogs they sell for the duration of each dog's life. to pet homes with spay/neuter contracts, whereby you agree as a condition of purchase to spay/neuter the dog you purchase. Good breeders care about the well-being of the dogs from their kennels for their entire lives. For the reasons listed above, as well as preventing lesser quality or older dogs from reproducing, they try to ensure that spaying/neutering takes place. This is a clear sign of a caring and concerned breeder, willing to risk a sale to ensure the future of the dog and the breed.

REGISTRATION

Any purebred Shar-Pei you purchase should be registerable with the American Kennel Club. Most times, the registration papers will be received upon final payment for the dog.

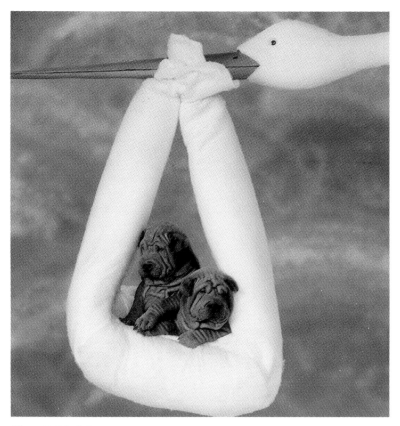

Shar-Pei babies are not delivered by a stork! Purchase your pup with registration papers that are complete with the registration numbers of the dog's parents.

Occasionally, by way of a written contract, the breeder will retain the papers until a condition (such as spaying/neutering, or producing a pick-of-litter pup) is met. The dog may also be "co-owned," meaning there is a shared ownership by the breeder or previous owner and yourself. It is vital, if you are not receiving the papers at the time you pick up the dog, that you have a written contract that clearly states when you *will* receive the papers. It is also preferable to get a copy of the dog's pedigree (likely to be handwritten) from the seller, and the registration numbers of the dog's parents. The more information you can get about your new companion, the better prepared you will be.

SOCIALIZATION

Animals, like children, need to be socialized. They need to learn to get along with a variety of people, in a variety of situations. A great start on this should take place wherever the pup is born. The more variety they are exposed to as pups, the more adaptable they will be as adults. In a controlled setting, the pup should be allowed to explore life! Keeping the pup safe is a major concern; you don't teach him to be confident on stairs by letting him fall down them! If you are active, have a great deal of company, or go places and do things, then you can take the puppy with you and he will experience new things as your companion! If he is likely to only leave the house when he goes to the veterinarian, then enroll him in a puppy socialization class, or make the time to take him to the park. Shar-Pei love travel and explore the world with their owners. Make it a consistent adventure, safe and fun, and your dog can be an even more complete companion!

Socialization with littermates will help teach your Shar-Pei puppy how to play fair—and when to stop! Puppies sure can play rough.

In addition to being a better companion, a well-socialized dog is more stable in temperament and can adjust to changes better (in case you suddenly have to leave town and have a stranger take care of the dog or leave the dog in a boarding kennel). Socialization removes fears and builds trust. It is, second to good veterinary care, the very best thing you can do for your dog, and for yourself.

When you bring home a new puppy, it is important to know what he has been used to. If he has slept in a crate at his former home, make sure he has a crate at your house. Keep the food the same, find out what his schedule was, etc. Learn as much about his life prior to coming home with you as possible, and then slowly integrate him into your life. I do not allow my puppies to become presents for holidays. This time is chaotic, with lots of paper tearing and much for the family to do. It is very unfair to make a puppy's first day in his new home one of confusion! Keep your schedule in mind when deciding when to take home your new dog. Find a time when you will be available to help him adjust to his new life.

PEDIGREES AND TITLES

While the various show phrases can be confusing, there are some easy to understand terms that you may find in your new dog's pedigree. Conformation Champion, abbreviated Ch., means that the dog has earned a championship based upon his looks and how closely he conforms to the ideal Shar-Pei described by the standard. CD stands for Companion Dog, a basic

Ch. Kim Lous Charmin Chang Bang is a multiple Group, Best of Breed and specialty winner. Owned by Sam and Kim Goza.

The author's accomplished Shar-Pei is Ch. Tai-Pan's Odie of Kasu, CD, TT, ROM, OFA, CERF. obedience title earned by going to obedience competitions (CDX, UD, UDX and OTCH are titles for even more difficult obedience competitions). TT is awarded by the Temperament Testing Society, which put the dogs through a ten step "test" and grades their temperament and socialization. OFA is the Orthopedic Foundation for Animals. OFA reviews x-rays of dogs and grades their hips and elbows, screening for hip dysplasia and other orthopedic problems. There are other abbreviations and titles as well, but the above are the most common. The breeder should make you aware of any titles earned by the dog or its parents/grandparents, as well as any examinations and health history.

GROWTH

Shar-Pei puppies grow very quickly, reaching near adult height by six to eight months of age. They will continue to bulk up through three years of age, but the height is determined prior to one year of age. (Shar-Pei average height is 18-20", with 16-21" being common. The average weight is 40 pounds for a small Shar-Pei to 60 pounds for a bigger dog.) While they reach their height quickly, it is important to remember they are still puppies and in need of puppy nutrition, but should never be allowed to become overweight as it will stress their joints.

Eventually, at about one year of age, or during their first spring season after six months of age, they will "blow coat." This is a shedding of the softer puppy coat, being replaced by a harsher adult coat. Many Shar-Pei go through this coat change annually, sometimes even changing the shade of their coat to a deeper or lighter hue. Because they have such short hair, you don't notice shedding much except during these periods. Some Shar-Pei, specifically horse coats, may look quite "moth eaten" during this time. If the skin looks healthy, with no redness or oozing, it's likely to be simple coat blow.

COAT TYPE

Shar-Pei come in three coat lengths, two of which are suitable to be shown. The horse coat is under one-half inch in length and is the shortest coat. Brush coats range between one half inch and one inch and have a bushier tail than the horse coat. The bear coat, which is any coat over one inch, is disqualified from the show ring. A puppy with this coat is most often sold as a pet on a spay/neuter contract so that it can not pass the coat length any further. All three are Shar-Pei, look like Shar-Pei, and act like Shar-Pei. You may find that you have a preference for one coat or another. The horse coat, while

being the Chinese preference, has been out of fashion for several years. Many breeders are now focusing their programs on resurrecting the horse coat

The horse coat is under one-half inch in length and is the shortest coat of the Shar-Pei. Felin's Chocolate Beau, TNT, displays a fine head.

The coat of a brush coat ranges between a half-inch and one-inch long and has a bushier tail than the horse coat. Wrinkling on the brush coat is harder to see than on the horse coat.

lines. Indeed, many feel that a horse coat is a "true" Shar-Pei!

It is harder to see the wrinkling on the brush coat, but they generally have a softer coat and a rounder look than the horse coat. Bear coats, while being any coat over one inch long, come in a variety of looks, from simply a furry brush coat look, to a true Chow look with a dense three-layered coat. Coat type is simply a matter of preference, so the more you see, the more obvious your choice will be.

COLOR

Nearly any color you might like can be found in the Shar-Pei world. In the standard for the breed, there is no preference in color, as long as it is solid. A spotted (sometimes called "flowered"), or multi-colored Shar-Pei is barred from the show ring. A list of colors can be found in the standard. As with many other aspects of this fascinating breed, the more colors you see, the better prepared you will be to make a choice.

PICKING THE IDEAL PUPPY

Once you have a clear notion of what it is you are looking for in quality, color, coat, etc., you are ready to begin the hands-on part (the *fun* part). You need to make one more clear decision in your head: what do you want the dog to do? If you want to work in obedience, you are looking for the slightly inquisitive, steady pup who watches you. If you want a calm companion for the family, don't pick the puppy who seems to be everywhere at once, jumping and barking and running! A feisty pup is likely to be a feisty adult; a cuddly pup, a cuddly adult. A timid pup means you will need to invest some energy in socializing; a rowdy pup will need definite play time. Watch them and distinguish their personalities, then pick one that comes closest to what you want to share your life with!

A Shar-Pei can be just about anything you want it to be. Pick the puppy that comes closest to what you want to share your life with.

Health-wise, the puppies should have clear eyes and alert dispositions, and should have had at least one set of shots (more if they are older than 10 to 12 weeks). Shar-Pei puppies may have had their eyes tacked (a suture is placed in the folds above and below the eye). As they are growing, their skin grows at a different rate than the rest of them, hence the wrinkles. Many times, when a pup is ten days old and due to open his eyes, these wrinkles press down heavily and make it impossible for him to get them open. A breeder will have the pup tacked within a few days if he doesn't grow into that wrinkle. To leave him basically blinded by that loose skin would damage his temperament. There are many who disagree on the seriousness of this procedure, some viewing it as "altering surgery" and making the dog ineligible for

Choose a Shar-Pei puppy with clear eyes and an alert disposition.

Two apricot dilute pups. The puppy on the right has his eyes tacked in order to correct a minor eye condition. the show ring. Others view it a temporary solution that does not alter the look of the dog after the sutures are removed. The important thing to remember is that it is a temporary, necessary procedure, and not cause for great alarm as to the future health of the puppy. However, many people will not sell a dog that has had its eyes tacked as show quality.

PREPARE FOR THE NEWCOMER

You've done your homework, you know what you want, you've found the ideal pup or adult, and you're ready to adopt a new family member. Before bringing the new one home, make sure you have taken care of the following:

1. Food. Make sure you have dog food on hand and read up on changing diets and feeding schedules. Having food on

hand eliminates a last minute rush to the grocery store, buying whatever is on sale.

2. Crate and/or baby gate. You will want some way to confine the new family member as he learns the house, family, and routine. Knowing what the newcomer is used to will help determine which of these items need to be purchased ahead of time.

3. Toys. The toys you purchase should be well thought out. Nylabones® are great for dogs of all ages and provide them with something safe to chew on. Rawhide chews have proven to be dangerous for many Shar-Pei as they chew them to a soggy mass and then attempt to swallow them whole, choking themselves or causing stomach problems. Cow hooves have also proven problematic as they may sliver and cause some internal problems.

The Nylafloss® proves to be a safe chew device that will provide your Shar-Pei with hours of fun. Only buy nylon rope toys— cotton is organic and rots.

You can take an old gym sock and tie a knot in the middle and you have a tug toy! Just remember that if you give your pup socks, stuffed toys, or old shoes, it may be hard for him to know the difference from your good socks, the kids' special stuffed animals and perfectly good shoes!

4. Veterinarian. If you already have a family veterinarian, check with him and see how knowledgeable he is about Shar-Pei. If your veterinarian rarely sees the breed, or if this is your first animal companion, you should check with your breeder or other Shar-Pei owners in the area and find a veterinarian familiar with the breed. It is also important to realize that most veterinarians know a great deal about dogs, but do not necessarily have a great understanding about particular breeds. It is unfair to expect a veterinarian to be able to confirm the quality of your dog,

since the veterinarian will likely have no knowledge of the breed standard or your dog's pedigree. Also, be prepared to make an appointment in the first week, because most sales contracts call for you to have the puppy checked by your veterinarian in the first few days, just to rule out any health problems the breeder may have been unaware of. If your usual veterinarian is inexperienced with Shar-Pei, but willing to learn all he needs to know to help you, then you've got a great start! If the veterinarian you choose is of the opinion that all Shar-Pei are bad tempered, in poor health, and should never have been bred...keep looking. Don't let one bad apple spoil your bushel of fun!

5. Time. Try to pick up your new pet when you will have plenty of time to help the newcomer adjust to the change. Perhaps picking the pup up on a Friday when you are off for the weekend, or some similar timing. The more attention you can devote to the new family member in the

Try to pick up your new Shar-Pei puppy early in the day so that he will have plenty of time to settle in and explore his new home.

Be sure to have all your new Shar-Pei's accessories—collar, lead, Nylabone®, crate, toys, bed, etc.,—ready and waiting for him on his arrival.

first few days, the sooner he will become a secure, comfortable member of your family.

6. Collar and Lead. The size collar you will get will depend on the age and size of the pup or dog you are bringing home. While there are many sizes and styles available, a good basic beginning would be a simple buckle collar and a 6-foot leather lead.

There are many, many decisions to be made in choosing the right Shar-Pei to share your life with. Begin by making sure that you want to share your life with a dog, and that you are ready for the responsibility. Then begin your lessons in learning all the wondrous variations of this most unusual breed!

After you've sorted through all the choices and made the decisions, prepare everything you can in advance to make the transition as smooth as possible. Well chosen, well prepared for, well trained and well loved is the Chinese Shar-Pei with whom life will be joyous and long lasting!

TRAINING and Housebreaking Your Shar-Pei

Whether training a Chinese Shar-Pei or another breed of dog, the main things to remember are *be consistent* and *be positive*. Dogs learn from positive reinforcement and from repetition. A good starting place is to realize that dogs think differently than humans:

A. Dogs have the instincts of being members of the pack. Your family (even if it is just you and your Shar-Pei) is the pack now. *You must be top dog.*

B. Dogs don't remember events the same way that humans do. If a dog has an accident at one o'clock, by the time you get home at five o'clock he often doesn't remember "making the mistake."

C. Dogs are much more comfortable with black and white; gray areas confuse them and require them to make decisions. Knowing that they could make the *wrong* decision causes them stress!

PRAISE, PRAISE, PRAISE!! Dogs will do *anything* for the people they love, and the only reward they require is our love. If you make training a *fun* and *enjoyable* experience, the dog will love doing it!

Praise your Shar-Pei until you both have a warm, fuzzy feeling.

BE CONSISTENT!! Dogs learn by repetition, both good and bad! If jumping on people is a "no," then it is *always* a "no." Only by being consistent in your training can you expect your dog to learn. If begging at the table is a "no" only half the time, then it is ALWAYS worth the risk!!

Kasu's Fast Action knows he is not supposed to be on the bed. Perhaps he is wondering why the "other dog is allowed.

Dogs do have "bad days" and they do seem to be affected by the full moon! If, when you go out to train one day, you know *you've* had a bad day, or your dog is just not his usual self, do an exercise the dog can perform, praise him, and call it a day. If your mind, or his mind, is not on the training, you can do more harm than good by letting

There will be days when your Shar-Pei will not want to train.

frustrations show. Remember, you and your dog are a team, partners in learning, and if one member of the team is not able to keep focused or concentrate, then the team can't function.

Discipline must be fair and quick! Once the undesired behavior is stopped, the discipline is stopped, and the praise begins! To berate or lecture won't work with a dog because he can't reason; he needs to know that putting the shoe in his mouth made you unhappy. When he got a loud "no," he dropped the shoe and suddenly you were very happy and he was getting a lot of love. Discipline *can* be a little sneaky: if Fido has developed a habit of barking at the fence, put some rocks in an empty soda can and throw it in his direction while he is barking (don't let him see you). What will go through his mind is, "I was barking at the fence, then suddenly, out of nowhere, this noisy thing came at me. When I don't bark at the fence, things don't come flying at me." From that, he can make the obvious doggie deduction! The trick with a surprise is that it should startle the dog, not hurt him.

You must catch the dog *in the act* in order to discipline! If you come home from work and Fido has destroyed the trash, he will "feel bad" if you holler about it. If the next day you come home and he has destroyed the trash again, he may act guilty, but what he is reacting to is either "she's home, I wonder if she'll holler like yesterday" or "somehow that mess is back and she'll be loud about it." The dog does not connect what it did three hours or ten minutes ago with the discipline he is receiving now! If Fido gets in trouble every time you come home and he doesn't have an understanding of *why*,

Puppies will be puppies and Shar-Pei are no exception. Know when to correct your misbehaving toddler.

very soon he'll dread having you come home! Don't let this happen. Catch him *in the act* so that he can make the connection!!

HOUSEBREAKING

Chinese Shar-Pei are not only extremely intelligent, they practically housebreak themselves! Raised in an environment that reinforces their natural desire to do their "business" as far from their bedroom and food as possible, they can be reliably house trained by six weeks of age. It is not unusual for a new puppy owner to take home an eight-

Shar-Pei are naturally clean and intelligent dogs that want to keep their living area clean. They practically housebreak themselves because they want to do their business as far from their food and bedroom as possible.

week-old Shar-Pei and call the breeder a week later to report that the puppy only had one accident, and that was because the new owner didn't let it outside quickly enough one morning! By and large, the major housebreaking adjustment a Shar-Pei will need is being familiar enough with his surroundings to know which door will be used to let him out.

To increase your success with housebreaking there are a few simple things to remember. First of all, puppies will need to eliminate right after they wake up from a nap, and usually after they eat a meal. Be speedy and watch the puppy. Every time you think the pup needs to go potty, take him outside. When he does what he's supposed to, outside, PRAISE him! As with all things, he learns housebreaking with praise and prompt correction. Should you see your new baby squat in the house, scoop him up with a quick, firm "no!" and take him outside immediately. He may be confused at first, but he will amaze you with how quickly he catches on!

Don't rub the puppy's nose in an accident. This confuses the puppy and is not very healthy. *Catch him in the act!* If you don't catch him, simply clean it up and keep a better eye on him. You need to catch him and correct him in order for the puppy to understand what you are trying to say.

BASIC OBEDIENCE

Basic obedience training is a must for owners and their dogs. It is much safer and more rewarding to have a trained dog, and the key is to train the owner so that the owner can train the dog. Find a good obedience school, one that teaches with praise, and enroll!

If you plan to do some of the training yourself, perhaps prior to a class, or if you live in an area where training classes are not offered, remember the lessons above. Be consistent and use praise! In being consistent while teaching obedience commands, the trick is to always use the same word for the

All dogs should be taught basic obedience commands. By teaching your Shar-Pei how to "sit," "come," and "off," you will both have a much happier life.

action. If you want your dog to get off the sofa, tell him "off." For my dogs, "off" means "get your feet off of whatever they are on," be it the sofa, my legs, or Grandma's lap! Always use the word "off" to mean the same thing, and be sure not to confuse it with "down." "Down" should mean "lay down." If you use the two words interchangeably, the dog will likely catch on some of the time, just by thinking about where he is and what your body language is telling him. But it is also going to be very confusing for the dog.

Imagine yourself in a new country where you don't understand a word of the language. Your hostess says "wock wock" and indicates a chair, so you sit. She smiles and you know you caught on. Then later she says, "nim nock ferd sock wock wock, tub rork sill wock?" You are totally confused! What she was really saying was, "Wouldn't you like to sit? Be a good visitor and sit?" Well, this is how your dog hears *you* talk! Dogs get along amazingly well in our world, but they really don't understand all the words in our sentences. Give them some help and keep the commands short and to the point. Help them out as they attempt to live in your world.

LEASH BREAKING

Leash breaking a puppy should be a gentle experience. Your safest route is to let him adjust to a collar for a couple of days. Then, while you are watching him closely, let him drag the leash attached to his collar around the house a few times a day

for 15 minutes or so. This helps the pup adjust to the weight and feel of the collar and lead.

When the puppy seems comfortable with the lead and collar, take the puppy to a new place, like a park, somewhere away from home. The puppy will be insecure in the new environment and will be more likely to follow you because you represent safety. This eliminates the need for tugging on the pup to get him go with you. Take your time. The puppy will quickly learn the limits of the leash, and the more fun places you take him, the more he will find the leash to be a sign of happiness!

With all experiences, whether leash breaking or riding in the car, your puppy will soon learn to enjoy them if they are fun and positive! If the only time your dog leaves the house is to go to the

Do not use your Shar-Pei's leash as a means of going to and from the veterinarian's office only. Use it for good experiences as well, such as a car ride or a walk in the park.

veterinarian once a year, he will not be likely to run to the car and jump in!

While a "choke" or training collar is preferred in actual obedience training classes, for use around the home your pet should wear a buckle collar. The training collars can strangle a dog quickly if they become hung up on anything. But remember to check the buckle collar often as the pup grows; you should have two fingers worth of room between the collar and the pup's neck.

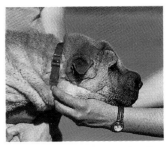

PULLING ON THE LEASH

So, you've trained the little wonder that the leash is a good thing and that the world is a fun place, and now he wants to drag you everywhere?! Try a quick jerk backwards and a loud "no pull" or "easy!" As soon as the leash is again loose between the two of you, *praise* him! A few 15-minute sessions of this and the dog will agree that walking is much more fun when there is no tugging and jerking going on! Just be consistent and be firm and then praise. You'll enjoy the walks more, too!

Buckle collars are safer for your Shar-Pei to wear while he is in the home or playing outdoors. Choke or training collars can easily become caught on something and should only be worn during obedience training classes.

FENCING

Fenced yards are a blessing and a necessity. While Shar-Pei are not runners or wanderers, any dog can be tempted. And unfortunately, Shar-Pei are stolen more often than they run away. Some people think the breed is still incredibly expensive, while others think they can be pit fighting dogs. In any event, a dog left unattended for long periods of time in a fenced yard is a target, and a loose dog, without the confines of a fence, is much more likely to meet a sad and untimely death. Protect your friend.

CRATE TRAINING

One of your first purchases should be a crate, whether a

plastic "airline crate" or a metal wire crate. You should purchase a crate big enough for a full grown Shar-Pei to be able to stand up straight and turn around. You can place the crate in the bedroom, the dining room, the kitchen, or whatever quiet, out of the way place you'd like the dog to sleep or relax in. You should have a nice rug in the bottom, a Nylabone® inside, and if you will leave the dog inside for any length of time, a water pan to hang on the door. I suggest feeding the dog his treats or perhaps even his meals in the crate.

A crate will make your Shar-Pei feel safe and should be regarded as a place he wants to go, not forced to go as punishment.

The crate should *not* be a place where bad dogs have to go, but rather should be a place for treats and quiet time. Make the crate a positive place and the dog will learn to enjoy its "bedroom."

It is very likely that the dog will be noisy the first few times you try to crate him. If you let him out because he is howling, he will always howl to get out! Don't give in. You can try one or more of the following: 1) Shar-Pei hate water, so keep a spray bottle nearby and squirt the howling dog in the face while saying "no"—only let the pup out when he is quiet. 2) Thunk the top of the crate with your hand while giving a loud "no!" Remember to give a soft, praising "good puppy" when the pup is quiet. 3) When the problem is that the pup can see you outside the crate, or maybe see the kids playing, try draping a towel over the front of the crate so that his line of sight is blocked. Never drape the entire crate because fresh air will be blocked.

Once a pup learns that he is not getting out every time

A baby's play-pen will keep your Shar-Pei pup confined while you are attending to chores. Do not leave him in there for any length of time as he may try to climb or chew his way out.

he makes a noise, and that he gets treats for being in his crate, he will settle in. After that, you just need to make sure that he gets some time in his crate each day, maybe at feeding time or overnight while you are sleeping, or perhaps while you are at work. Overnight, he will sleep quietly in his crate. If the puppy is going to be crated during a normal play time, make sure that you leave a Nylabone® or some other safe toy inside to give the pup something to do.

CAR RIDES

The safest place in your car for your Shar-Pei is either in a crate or with a seat-belt harness on. Like small children, the dog can become a flying projectile during a sudden stop and can come to a tragic end during a fun outing! It is also not a good idea to let your dog hang his head out the window while riding. The wind can blow foreign objects into his eyes and ears. And never, never leave your Shar-Pei in a hot car or let him ride in the back of an open-bed pickup truck! Practical sense, planning ahead, and making the rides fun but safe are your best choices.

It is not safe to allow your Shar-Pei to ride unrestricted in a car or van. The best place for him is in a traveling crate or with a seat-belt harness on.

BABY GATES

Baby gates, available at most hardware and discount stores, are wonderful for limiting the dog's access to parts of the house, or blocking him in the spaces he is welcome. The gates can be extended to fit various doorways and give the dog room and space, while limiting his ability to get into trouble!

Shar-Pei are not runners or wanderers, however, any dog can be tempted while outdoors. Fenced yards are not only a blessing, they are a necessity.

In all areas of training, remember the basics of consistency and praise. Be practical and considerate and plan ahead. The more preparations you make, the safer and more fun life with your Shar-Pei will be!

CARING for Your Shar-Pei

The Chinese Shar-Pei is an "easy keeper" breed, meaning that the typical, healthy Shar-Pei requires little specialized care. In this section, references to puppies will usually mean dogs under one year of age. The basic ingredient for any dog's diet will be good dry dog food. Whether you get a puppy or an adult, it should already be used to a good dry food. If you are going to change brands of dog food, you should do so gradually so as not to upset your dog's digestive system. Usually this can be done by mixing one-fourth of the new food with three-fourths of the former food for the first two days; then two days of half new food and half former food; and finally two days of three-fourths new and one-fourth former.

Given the proper blend of exercise, good nutrition, suitable housing, and routine veterinary care, your Shar-Pei can be expected to be an active member of your household for many years.

Each breeder will have his own preference in brands of dog food, but a good rule to follow is to stick with a nationally advertised brand. Major brands of dog food meet federal guidelines but in addition carry certification on their labels that they have passed necessary requirements. The producers of these major brands conduct ongoing testing of their foods, making sure they are nutritionally sound and that dogs like the taste. Since the dry food will be the major source of nutrition for your Shar-Pei, you will want to make sure that it is safe and well-tested. Contrary to some old theories, Shar-Pei do not seem to have a problem with soy-based foods. While all breeds will have an occasional dog with some type of food allergy, most Shar-Pei do well on any quality, name brand food. You should read labels and make sure you are not loading the dog with too much fat or protein and that you are keeping a good balance; most major brands clearly label their food as "high protein," etc.

You can add some canned food, again produced by a major company; however, feeding only soft or canned food is not

more expensive, and more likely to cause tooth decay. Using canned food in moderation, as an occasional treat, is certainly fine.

Puppies should be fed more frequently than adults because although they have smaller stomachs, they need more food for their growth. Feed pups three times a day until four months of age, two times a day until at least six months of age, and after that move on to adult instructions. (Leave them on *puppy* food until one year of age.) Adults can be fed once or twice a day, or you can leave dry food down at all times for free feeding. If you find your dog is an overeater when food is always available, you should limit the intake by feeding limited amounts twice a day (usually a cup or two at a time). If you don't intend to free feed, you should consider feeding them in their crate. They can eat their food in the privacy of their "hotel room." You should keep an eye on how much they eat, if for no other reason than to be alert to any changes in their eating habits, a helpful hint for your veterinarian in case your dog is ever ill.

Always have fresh water available. This is the single most important thing you can do for your dog! And, as with food, your veterinarian may need to ask if your dog is drinking more water than usual, so keep an eye on what is "normal" for your Shar-Pei.

Veterinary medicine has become far more sophisticated than what was available to our ancestors. This can be attributed to the increase in household pets and consequently the demand for better care for them. Also human medicine has become far more complex. Today diagnostic testing in veterinary medicine parallels human diagnostics. Because of better technology we can expect our pets to live healthier lives thereby increasing their life spans.

THE FIRST CHECK UP

You will want to take your new puppy/dog in for its first check up within 48 to 72 hours after acquiring it. Many breeders strongly recommend this check up and so do the humane shelters. A puppy/dog can appear healthy but it may have a serious problem that is not apparent to the layman. Most pets have some type of a minor flaw that may never cause a real problem.

Unfortunately if he/she should have a serious problem, you

will want to consider the consequences of keeping the pet and the attachments that will be formed, which may be broken prematurely. Keep in mind there are many healthy dogs looking for good homes.

This first check up is a good time to establish yourself with the veterinarian and learn the office policy regarding their hours and how they handle emergencies. Usually the breeder or another conscientious pet owner is a good reference for locating a capable veterinarian. You should be aware that not all veterinarians give the same quality of service. Please do not make your selection on the least expensive clinic, as they may be short changing your pet. There is the possibility that eventually it will cost you more due to improper diagnosis, treatment, etc. If you are selecting a new veterinarian, feel free to ask for a tour of the clinic. You should inquire about making an appointment for a tour since all clinics are working

A dog-owning friend or a breeder will be the best source for finding a veterinarian.

clinics, and therefore may not be available all day for sightseers. You may worry less if you see where your pet will be spending the day if he ever needs to be hospitalized.

THE PHYSICAL EXAM

Your veterinarian will check your pet's overall condition, which includes listening to the heart; checking the respiration; feeling the abdomen, muscles and joints; checking the mouth, which includes the gum color and signs of gum disease along with plaque buildup; checking the ears for signs of an infection or ear mites; examining the eyes; and, last but not least, checking the condition of the skin and coat.

He should ask you questions regarding your pet's eating and elimination habits and invite you to relay your questions. It is a good idea to prepare a list so as not to forget anything. He should discuss the proper diet and the quantity to be fed. If this should differ from your breeder's recommendation, then you should convey to him the breeder's choice and see if he approves. If he recommends changing the diet, then this should be done over a few days so as not to cause a gastrointestinal upset. It is customary to take in a fresh stool sample (just a small amount) for a test for intestinal parasites. It must be fresh, preferably within 12 hours, since the eggs hatch quickly and after hatching will not be observed under the microscope. If your pet isn't obliging then, usually the technician can take one in the clinic.

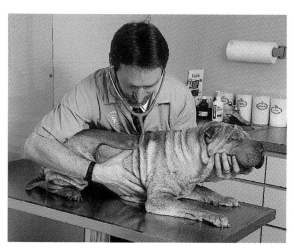

Your Shar-Pei should have a physical exam performed by the veterinarian at least once a year to check his overall condition.

IMMUNIZATIONS

It is important that you take your puppy/dog's vaccination record with you on your first visit. In case of a puppy, presumably the breeder has seen to the vaccinations up to the time you acquired custody. Veterinarians differ in their vaccination protocol. It is not unusual for your puppy to have received vaccinations for

Your Shar-Pei puppy will require a series of vaccinations that may have been started by the breeder.

distemper, hepatitis, leptospirosis, parvovirus and parainfluenza every two to three weeks from the age of five or six weeks. Usually this is a combined injection and is typically called the DHLPP. The DHLPP is given through at least 12 to 14 weeks of age, and it is customary to continue with another parvovirus vaccine at 16 to

Plan a trip to the veterinarian soon after you bring your new Shar-Pei puppy home. Regular physical exams will ensure your dog a happy and healthy life.

18 weeks. You may wonder why so many immunizations are necessary. No one knows for sure when the puppy's maternal antibodies are gone, although it is customarily accepted that distemper antibodies are gone by 12 weeks. Usually parvovirus antibodies are gone by 16 to 18 weeks of age. However, it is possible for the maternal antibodies to be gone at a much earlier age or even a later age. Therefore immunizations are started at an early age. The vaccine will not give immunity as long as there are maternal antibodies.

The rabies vaccination is given at three or six months of age depending on your local laws. A vaccine for bordetella (kennel cough) is advisable and can be given anytime from the age of five weeks. The coronavirus is not commonly given unless there is a problem locally. The Lyme vaccine is necessary in endemic areas. Lyme disease has been reported in 47 states.

Distemper

This is virtually an incurable disease. If the dog recovers, he is subject to severe nervous disorders. The virus attacks every tissue in the body and resembles a bad cold with a fever. It can cause a runny nose and eyes and cause gastrointestinal disorders, including a poor appetite, vomiting and diarrhea. The virus is carried by raccoons, foxes, wolves, mink and other dogs. Unvaccinated youngsters and senior citizens are very susceptible. This is still a common disease.

Maternal antibodies can last in a pup believably for 12 to 18 weeks. Nevertheless, immunizations should begin when the pup is between six and eight weeks.

70

Hepatitis

This is a virus that is most serious in very young dogs. It is spread by contact with an infected animal or its stool or urine. The virus affects the liver and kidneys and is characterized by high fever, depression and lack of appetite. Recovered animals may be afflicted with chronic illnesses.

Bordetella attached to canine cilia, otherwise known as kennel cough, is a highly contagious disease and should be vaccinated against routinely.

Leptospirosis

This is a bacterial disease transmitted by contact with the urine of an infected dog, rat or other wildlife. It produces severe symptoms of fever, depression, jaundice and internal bleeding and was fatal before the vaccine was developed. Recovered dogs can be carriers, and the disease can be transmitted from dogs to humans.

Parvovirus

This was first noted in the late 1970s and is still a fatal disease. However, with proper vaccinations, early diagnosis and prompt treatment, it is a manageable disease. It attacks the bone marrow and intestinal tract. The symptoms include depression, loss of appetite, vomiting, diarrhea and collapse. Immediate medical attention is of the essence.

Rabies

This is shed in the saliva and is carried by raccoons, skunks, foxes, other dogs and cats. It attacks nerve tissue, resulting in paralysis and death. Rabies can be transmitted to people and is virtually always fatal. This disease is reappearing in the suburbs.

Bordetella (Kennel Cough)

The symptoms are coughing, sneezing, hacking and retching accompanied by nasal discharge usually lasting from a few days to several weeks. There are several disease-producing organisms responsible for this disease. The present vaccines are helpful but do not protect for all the strains. It usually is not life threatening but in some instances it can progress to a serious bronchopneumonia. The disease is highly contagious. The vaccination should be given routinely for dogs that come in contact with other dogs, such as through boarding, training class or visits to the groomer.

Coronavirus

This is usually self limiting and not life threatening. It was first noted in the late '70s about a year before parvovirus. The virus produces a yellow/brown stool and there may be depression, vomiting and diarrhea.

Small tight ears, as the Shar-Pei possesses, are susceptible to ear mites and infections due to the lack of air circulation. It is therefore important that you have these checked regularly.

Lyme Disease

This was first diagnosed in the United States in 1976 in Lyme, CT in people who lived in close proximity to the deer tick. Symptoms may include acute lameness, fever, swelling of joints and loss of appetite. Your veterinarian can advise you if you live in an endemic area.

After your puppy has completed his puppy vaccinations, you will continue to booster the DHLPP once a year. It is customary to booster the rabies one year after the first vaccine and then, depending on where you live, it should be boostered every year or every three years. This depends on your local laws. The Lyme and corona vaccines are boostered annually and it is recommended that the bordetella be boostered every six to eight months.

ANNUAL VISIT

I would like to impress the importance of the annual check up, which would include the booster vaccinations, check for intestinal parasites and test for heartworm. Today in our very busy world it is rush, rush and see "how much you can get for how little." Unbelievably, some non-veterinary businesses have entered into the vaccination business. More harm than good can come to your dog through improper vaccinations, possibly from inferior vaccines and/or the wrong schedule. More than

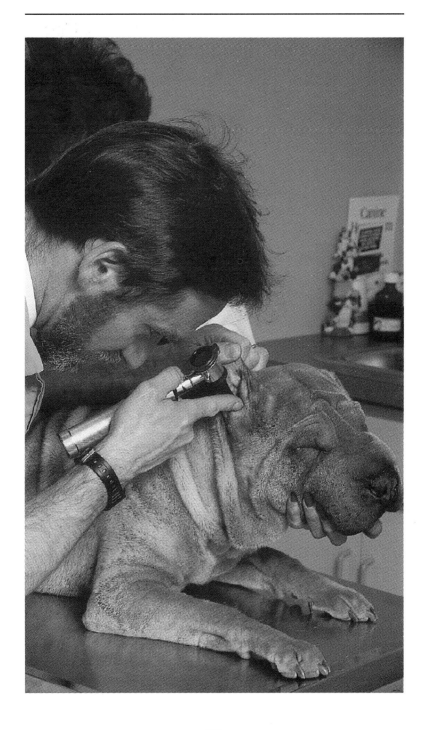

likely you truly care about your companion dog and over the years you have devoted much time and expense to his well being. Perhaps you are unaware that a vaccination is not just a vaccination. There is more involved. Please, please follow through with regular physical examinations. It is so important for your veterinarian to know your dog and this is especially true during middle age through the geriatric years. More than likely your older dog will require more than one physical a year. The annual physical is good preventive medicine. Through early diagnosis and subsequent treatment your dog can maintain a longer and better quality of life.

INTESTINAL PARASITES

Hookworms

These are almost microscopic intestinal worms that can cause anemia and therefore serious problems, including death, in young puppies. Hookworms can be transmitted to

Hookworms are macroscopic intestinal worms that can cause anemia and other serious problems, including death.

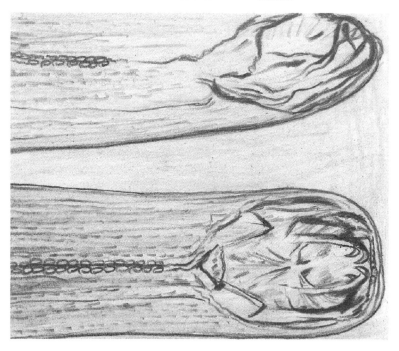

humans through penetration of the skin. Puppies may be born with them.

Roundworms

These are spaghetti-like worms that can cause a potbellied appearance and dull coat along with more severe symptoms, such as vomiting, diarrhea and coughing. Puppies acquire these while in the mother's uterus and through lactation. Both hookworms and roundworms may be acquired through ingestion.

Whipworms

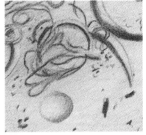

These have a three-month life cycle and are not acquired through the dam. They cause intermittent diarrhea usually with mucus. Whipworms are possibly the most difficult worm to eradicate. Their eggs are very resistant to most environmental factors and can last for years until the proper conditions enable them to mature. Whipworms are seldom seen in the stool.

Whipworms are hard to find unless one strains the feces, and this is best left to a veterinarian. Pictured here are adult whipworms.

Intestinal parasites are more prevalent in some areas than others. Climate, soil and contamination are big factors contributing to the incidence of intestinal parasites. Eggs are passed in the stool, lay on the ground and then become infective in a certain number of days. Each of the above worms has a different life cycle. Your best chance of becoming and remaining worm-free is to always pooper-scoop your yard. A fenced-in yard keeps stray dogs out, which is certainly helpful.

I would recommend having a fecal examination on your dog twice a year or more often if there is a problem. If your dog has a positive fecal sample, then he will be given the appropriate medication and you will be asked to bring back another stool sample in a certain period of time (depending on the type of worm) and then be rewormed. This process goes on until he has at least two negative samples. The different types of worms require different medications. You will be wasting your money

and doing your dog an injustice by buying over-the-counter medication without first consulting your veterinarian.

Coccidiosis and Giardiasis

These protozoal infections usually affect puppies, especially in places where large numbers of puppies are brought together. Older dogs may harbor these infections but do not show signs unless they are stressed. Symptoms include diarrhea, weight loss and lack of appetite. These infections are not always apparent in the fecal examination.

Tapeworms

Seldom apparent on fecal floatation, they are diagnosed frequently as rice-like segments around the dog's anus and the base of the tail. Tapeworms are long, flat and ribbon like, sometimes several feet in length, and made up of many segments about five-eighths of an inch long. The two most common types of tapeworms found in the dog are:

The energy level of Shar-Pei varies from dog to dog. In a multi-dog household, competition incites play, appetite and bonding.

(1) First the larval form of the flea tapeworm parasite must mature in an intermediate host, the flea, before it can become infective. Your dog acquires this by ingesting the flea through licking and chewing.

(2) Rabbits, rodents and certain large game animals serve as intermediate hosts for other species of tapeworms. If your dog should eat one of these infected hosts, then he can acquire tapeworms.

The more time your Shar-Pei spends outdoors, the more chances he has of picking up parasites. Make sure to check for both internal and external parasites often.

This is a worm that resides in the heart and adjacent blood vessels of the lung that produces microfilaria, which circulate in the bloodstream. It is possible for a dog to be infected with any number of worms from one to a hundred that can be 6 to 14 inches long. It is a life-threatening disease, expensive to treat and easily prevented. Depending on where you live, your veterinarian may recommend a preventive year-round and either an annual or semiannual blood test. The most common preventive is given once a month.

EXTERNAL PARASITES

Fleas

These pests are not only the dog's worst enemy but also enemy to the owner's pocketbook. Preventing is less expensive than treating, but regardless I think we'd prefer to spend our money elsewhere. I would guess that the majority of our dogs are allergic to the bite of a flea, and in many cases it only takes one flea bite. The protein in the flea's saliva is the culprit. Allergic dogs have a reaction, which usually results in a "hot spot." More than likely such a reaction will involve a trip to the veterinarian for treatment. Yes, prevention is less expensive. Fortunately today there are several good products available.

If there is a flea infestation, no one product is going to correct the problem. Not only will the dog require treatment so will the environment. In general flea collars are not very effective although there is now available an "egg" collar that will kill the eggs on the dog. Dips are the most economical but they are messy. There are some effective shampoos and treatments available through pet shops and veterinarians. An oral tablet arrived on the American market in 1995 and was popular in Europe the previous year. It sterilizes the female flea but will not kill adult fleas. Therefore the tablet, which is given monthly, will decrease the flea population but is not a "cure-all." Those dogs that suffer from flea-bite allergy will still be subjected to the bite of the flea. Another popular parasiticide is permethrin, which is applied to the back of the dog in one or two places depending on the dog's weight. This product works as a repellent causing the flea to get "hot feet" and jump off. Do not confuse this product with some of the organophosphates that are also applied to the dog's back.

Some products are not usable on young puppies. Treating fleas should be done under your veterinarian's guidance. Frequently it is necessary to combine products and the layman does not have the knowledge regarding possible toxicities. It is hard to believe but there are a few dogs that do have a natural resistance to fleas. Nevertheless it would be wise to treat all pets at the same time. Don't forget your cats. Cats just love to prowl the neighborhood and consequently return with unwanted guests.

The deer tick is the most common carrier of Lyme disease. Photo courtesy of Virbac Laboratories, Inc., Fort Worth, Texas.

Adult fleas live on the dog but their eggs drop off the dog into the environment. There they go through four larval stages before reaching adulthood, and thereby are able to jump back on the poor unsuspecting dog. The cycle resumes and takes between 21 to 28 days under ideal conditions. There are environmental products available that will kill both the adult fleas and the larvae.

Ticks

Ticks carry Rocky Mountain Spotted Fever, Lyme disease and can cause tick paralysis. They should be removed with tweezers, trying to pull out the head. The jaws carry disease. There is a tick preventive collar that does an excellent job. The ticks automatically back out on those dogs wearing collars.

Sarcoptic Mange

This is a mite that is difficult to find on skin scrapings. The pinnal reflex is a good indicator of this disease. Rub the ends of the pinna (ear) together and the dog will start scratching with his foot. Sarcoptes are highly contagious to other dogs and to humans although they do not live long on humans. They cause intense itching.

Demodectic Mange

This is a mite that is passed from the dam to her puppies. It affects youngsters age three to ten months. Diagnosis is confirmed by skin scraping. Small areas of alopecia around the eyes, lips and/or forelegs become visible. There is little itching unless there is a secondary bacterial infection. Some breeds are afflicted more than others.

Cheyletiella

This causes intense itching and is diagnosed by skin scraping. It lives in the outer layers of the skin of dogs, cats, rabbits and humans. Yellow-gray scales may be found on the back and the rump, top of the head and the nose.

Breeders put a lot of time and energy into producing top-quality puppies. Pictured here is an entire litter of apricot dilute pups.

TO BREED OR NOT TO BREED

More than likely your breeder has requested that you have your puppy neutered or spayed. Your breeder's request is based on what is healthiest for your dog and what is most beneficial for your breed. Experienced and conscientious breeders devote many years into developing a bloodline. In order to do this, he makes every effort to plan each breeding in regard to conformation, temperament and health. This type of breeder does his best to perform the necessary testing (i.e., OFA, CERF, testing for inherited blood disorders, thyroid, etc.). Testing is expensive and sometimes very disheartening when a favorite dog doesn't pass his health tests. The health history pertains not only to the breeding stock but to the immediate ancestors. Reputable breeders do not want their offspring to be bred indiscriminately. Therefore you may be asked to neuter or spay your puppy. Of course there is always the exception, and your

The health history of the breeding stock, as well as the immediate ancestors is taken into account. If these are clear of hereditary problems, a breeding will take place.

breeder may agree to let you breed your dog under his direct supervision. This is an important concept. More and more effort is being made to breed healthier dogs.

Spay/Neuter

There are numerous benefits of performing this surgery at six months of age. Unspayed females are subject to mammary and ovarian cancer. In order to prevent mammary cancer she must be spayed prior to her first heat cycle. Later in life, an unspayed female may develop a pyometra (an infected uterus), which is definitely life threatening.

Spaying is performed under a general anesthetic and is easy on the young dog. As you might expect it is a little harder on the older dog, but that is no reason to deny her the surgery. The surgery removes the ovaries and uterus. It is important to remove all the ovarian tissue. If some is left behind, she could remain attractive to males. In order to view the ovaries, a

These two Shar-Pei are simply playing around, however, hormonal aggressiveness, can be lessened by neutering at a young age.

reasonably long incision is necessary. An ovariohysterectomy is considered major surgery.

Neutering the male at a young age will inhibit some characteristic male behavior that owners frown upon. I have found my boys will not hike their legs and mark territory if they are neutered at six months of age. Also neutering at a young age has hormonal benefits, lessening the chance of hormonal aggressiveness.

Surgery involves removing the testicles but leaving the scrotum. If there should be a retained testicle, then he definitely needs to be neutered before the age of two or three years. Retained testicles can develop into cancer. Unneutered males are at risk for testicular cancer, perineal fistulas, perianal tumors and fistulas and prostatic disease.

Intact males and females are prone to housebreaking accidents. Females urinate frequently before, during and after heat cycles, and males tend to mark territory if there is a female in heat. Males may show the same behavior if there is a visiting dog or guests.

Surgery involves a sterile operating procedure equivalent to human surgery. The incision site is shaved, surgically scrubbed and draped. The veterinarian wears a sterile surgical gown, cap, mask and gloves. Anesthesia should be monitored by a registered technician. It is customary for the veterinarian to recommend a pre-anesthetic blood screening, looking for metabolic problems and a ECG rhythm strip to check for normal heart function. Today anesthetics are equal to human anesthetics, which enables your dog to walk out of the clinic the same day as surgery.

It is an old wives' tale that a dog will gain weight after being spayed or neutered. The fact is that most Shar-Pei are just as active after surgery as they were before.

Some folks worry about their dog gaining weight after being neutered or spayed. This is usually not the case. It is true that some dogs may be less active so they could develop a problem, but my own dogs are just as active as they were before surgery. I have a hard time keeping weight on them. However, if your dog should begin to gain, then you need to decrease his food and see to it that he gets a little more exercise.

THYROID

Thyroid deficiency is common in Shar-Pei. Signs are loss of hair, darkening of skin, loss of or large increase in appetite, lethargy, inactive sperm, and seeking out warmth. If your veterinarian runs a thyroid test and your dog is "low normal," it is a good idea to put him on medication. Shar-Pei seem to test differently than other breeds. Some Shar-Pei seem to need a thyroid "boost" during their adolescence. Many have needed medication for six months or so, but then their own thyroid seemed to kick back in.

ANAL SACS

These are small sacs on either side of the rectum that can cause the dog discomfort when they are full. They should empty when the dog has a bowel movement. Symptoms of inflammation or impaction are excessive licking under the tail and/or a bloody or sticky discharge from the anal area.

Breeders like myself recommend emptying the sacs on a regular schedule when bathing the dog. Many veterinarians prefer this isn't done unless there are symptoms. You can express the sacs by squeezing the two sacs (at the five

Many Shar-Pei seem to need a thyroid boost during their adolescence. They stay on medication for six months or so, and then their own thyroid kicks back in.

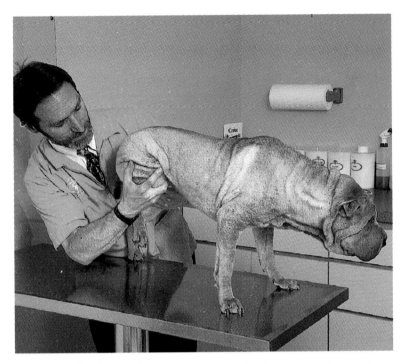

Occasionally the anal sacs will need to be expressed. If your Shar-Pei is scooting across the floor or licking his rear, it is time to visit the veterinarian. and seven o'clock positions) in and up toward the anus. Take precautions not to get in the way of the foul-smelling fluid that is expressed. Some dogs object to this procedure so it would be wise to have someone hold the head. Scooting is caused by anal-sac irritation and not worms.

COLITIS

The stool may be frank blood or blood tinged and is the result of inflammation of the colon. Colitis, sometimes intermittent, can be the result of stress, undiagnosed whipworms, or perhaps idiopathic (no explainable reason). I have had several dogs prone to this disorder. They felt fine and were willing to eat but would have intermittent bloody stools. If this in an ongoing problem, you should probably feed a diet higher in fiber. Seek professional help if your dog feels poorly and/or the condition persists.

EYES

Many times, during humid summer days or blooming spring days, your dog's eyes may look "gooby" with a yellowish or greenish mucous-like discharge in the corners. This is likely to be a very slight allergy and no cause for alarm. You can simply take a damp cloth and wipe the discharge away, or you can flush the dog's eyes with a human saline eye wash. As long as the dog is opening his eyes and the eyeball is clear, you have no reason to worry. If you notice any cloudiness on the eye, or if the dog is constantly squinting or blinking, take the dog to the veterinarian. If you are not confident that your veterinarian is familiar with Shar-Pei eyes, we recommend that you find a veterinarian experienced in this area. *Avoid having your veterinarian perform surgery, especially if the dog is under one year of age, and, in any case, make sure your veterinarian knows Shar-Pei eyes!* This is stressed because, as a pup grows, the shape of his head and face will change. A pup that has entropion surgery will many times grow into an adult with a permanently surprised look on his face! It is easy to remove too much skin from around the eye, leaving the dog to grow into, and stretch, the eye skin into a surprised look. For this reason, an experienced veterinarian is a necessity, as is patience.

Conjunctivitis

Many breeds are prone to this problem. The conjunctiva is the pink tissue that lines the inner surface of the eyeball except the clear, transparent cornea. Irritating substances such as bacteria, foreign matter or chemicals can cause it to become

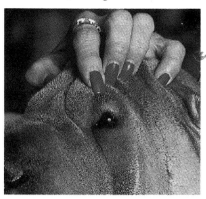

reddened and swollen. It is important to keep any hair trimmed from around the eyes. Long hair stays damp and aggravates the problem. Keep the eyes cleaned with

It is important that you keep any obstructions such as long hairs or foreign particles from your Shar-Pei's eyes. Irritating substances can cause problems.

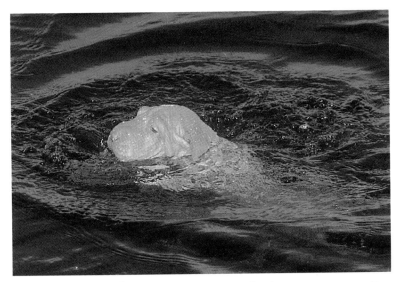

Swimming is excellent exercise for Shar-Pei. Be sure that you check the ears after swimming to avoid an infection setting in.

warm water and wipe away any matter that has accumulated in the corner of the eyes. If the condition persists, you should see your veterinarian. This problem goes hand in hand with keratoconjunctivitis sicca.

EARS

Like all breeds, Shar-Pei need to have their ears cleaned periodically. Many commercial products are available for this purpose. The place always to begin is with cotton tip swabs, gently cleaning the outer ear. Wax build up and some dirt is normal. Black and waxy discharge, yellow discharge, or reddish discharge is not typical and should be seen by your veterinarian. It is not uncommon for a Shar-Pei with extremely small ears and ear canals to experience occasional yeast or other types of infections. These are easily handled by a veterinarian.

Ear Infection

Otitis externa is an inflammation of the external ear canal that begins at the outside opening of the ear and extends inward to the eardrum. Dogs with pendulous ears are prone to this disease, but isn't it interesting that breeds with upright ears also have a high incidence of problems? Allergies, food and inhalent, along with hormonal problems, such as hypothyroidism, are major contributors to the disease. For those dogs which have recurring problems you need to investigate the underlying cause if you hope to cure them.

I recommend that you are careful never to get water into the ears. Water provides a great medium for bacteria to grow. If your dog swims or you inadvertently get water into his ears, then use a drying agent. An at-home preparation would be to use equal parts of three-percent hydrogen peroxide and 70-percent rubbing alcohol. Another *Be careful when cleaning your Shar-Pei's ears with cotton swabs. These make it easy to pack debris down into the ear canal.*

preparation is equal parts of white vinegar and water. Your veterinarian alternatively can provide a suitable product. When cleaning the ears, be careful of using cotton tip applicators since they make it easy to pack debris down into the canal. Only clean what you can see.

If your dog has an ongoing infection, don't be surprised if your veterinarian recommends sedating him and flushing his ears with a bulb syringe. Sometimes this needs to be done a few times to get the ear clean. The ear must be clean so that medication can come in contact with the canal. Be prepared to return for rechecks until the infection is gone. This may involve more flushings if the ears are very bad.

For chronic or recurring cases, your veterinarian may recommend thyroid testing, etc., and a hypoallergenic diet for a trial period of 10 to 12 weeks. Depending on your dog, it may be a good idea to see a dermatologist. Ears shouldn't be

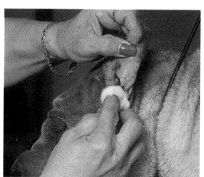

taken lightly. If the condition gets out of hand, then surgery may be necessary. Please ask your veterinarian to explain proper ear maintenance for your dog.

Shar-Pei are prone to ear problems. Your veterinarian will be able to advise you on the proper ear maintenance for your Shar-Pei.

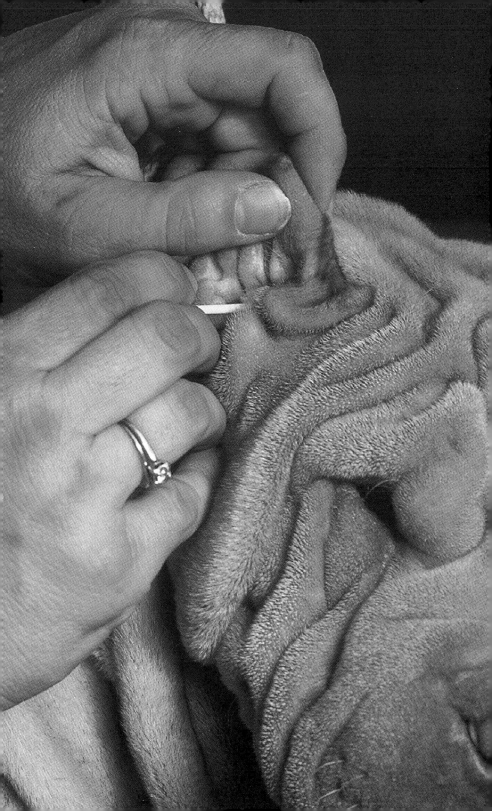

ALLERGIC REACTIONS

Slight flea allergies and minor allergic reactions to pollen or insect bites can be annoying, but can be easily handled with an antihistamine or a similar product from your veterinarian. *Beware*: Some dogs have severe reactions to insect stings! This will progress from scratching to hives to perhaps swelling of the nasal passages. At this point, the dog's life may be in danger and you should immediately take the dog to the veterinarian.

ANESTHETICS

Shar-Pei react poorly to many common anesthetics. We recommend discussing this with your veterinarian before any surgery so that your veterinarian has time to prepare and to do some research if necessary.

FEET

All dogs need their nails cut on a regular basis. Clipping or grinding are both successful means. Start working with your dog's feet as soon as you bring him home! Do not fight, do not struggle. Begin working with one toe at a time. If you cut too closely to the dog's vein ("quick") and the dog bleeds, you can try an iodine/water mix or a prepared blood clotting powder. Always be very cautious with the nails so they do not get infected. Although I have not personally done this, a friend uses a rasp file—she and her dogs like this way best! The dogs lay in her lap while she files their nails!

Interdigital Cysts

Check for these on your dog's feet if he shows signs of lameness. They are frequently associated with staph infections and can be quite painful. A home remedy is to soak the infected foot in a solution of a half teaspoon of bleach in a couple of quarts of water. Do this two to three times a day for a couple of days. Check with your veterinarian for an alternative remedy; antibiotics usually work well. If there is a recurring problem, surgery may be required.

Lameness

It may only be an interdigital cyst or it could be a mat between the toes, especially if your dog licks his feet.

The comfort of

having a friend

MAY BE TAKEN AWAY -
BUT NOT THE COMFORT OF HAVING HAD ONE.

A contribution to the University of Pennsylvania
School of Veterinary Medicine has been made by

Dr + Mrs Joseph Nebrudoshie

in memory of

Lue Blue Fredd

This donation supports the Matthew J. Ryan Veterinary Hospital
of the University of Pennsylvania, a leader in the development of
new treatments and technologies to improve the health and care
of companion animals.

One of the largest and most advanced companion animal teaching hospitals in the world, the Matthew J. Ryan Veterinary Hospital of the University of Pennsylvania sees more than 30,000 patient visits per year, including 13,000 through the Emergency Service. As part of the University of Pennsylvania School of Veterinary Medicine, the Ryan Veterinary Hospital is at the forefront of training students and veterinarians in the diagnosis and treatment of animal diseases. For more information on the Ryan Veterinary Hospital, visit the school's web site at www.vet.upenn.edu.

Penn
Veterinary Medicine

Many Species. One Medicine.™

Sometimes it is hard to determine which leg is affected. If he is holding up his leg, then you need to see your veterinarian.

SKIN

Frequently poor skin is the result of an allergy to fleas, an inhalant allergy or food allergy. These types of problems usually result in a staph dermatitis. Dogs with food allergy usually show signs of severe itching and scratching. However, I have had some dogs with food allergies that never once itched. Their only symptom was swelling of the ears with no ear infection. Food allergy may result in recurrent bacterial skin and ear infections. Your veterinarian or dermatologist will recommend a good restricted diet. It is not wise for you to hit and miss with different dog foods. Many of the diets offered over the counter are not the hypoallergenic diet you are led to believe. Dogs acquire allergies through exposure.

Accustom your Shar-Pei puppy to having his nails trimmed on a regular basis. Start working with your dog's feet as soon as you bring him home.

Inhalant allergies result in atopy, which causes licking of the feet, scratching the body and rubbing the muzzle. It may be seasonable. Your veterinarian or dermatologist can

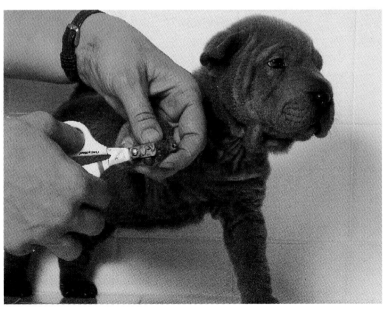

perform intradermal testing for inhalant allergies. If your dog should test positive, then a vaccine may be prepared. The results are very satisfying.

SHAR-PEI SWOLLEN HOCK SYNDROME

This is an unusual "fever of unknown origin" illness that is currently part of the research being conducted on amyloidosis. Funded by breeders and the by the Chinese Shar-Pei Club of America (CSPCA), this research is being conducted at Cornell University. Swollen hock syndrome often precedes amyloidosis, but we have no definitive answers yet. It is typified by a tender or stiff hock (ankle) joint and a sudden high fever. The fever is universal to the disease; however, the face or some other joint can swell and become tender in less common instances. Your veterinarian will not be able to identify any specific problem. He will usually prescribe antibiotics and something to break the fever, perhaps even a steroid. By the next day, your Shar-Pei will be fine, acting as if nothing unusual occurred the day before. These fevers are often recurring incidents, and their frequency varies greatly. One thing you may notice is that after any fever, a Shar-Pei has the loss of some of its facial padding. Shar-Pei muzzles are made up of a great deal of water and a fever will cause the fluid levels to drop, hence the face will shrink! (It will return; however, the time that it takes can vary from a week to several months.)

Be careful where you exercise your Shar-Pei. Chemicals used on lawns and fields may cause an allergic reaction in your dog—especially if he has sensitive feet.

CUTS AND PUNCTURES

Always keep plenty of triple antibiotic ointment on hand! Clean a puncture out with an iodine disinfectant, then squeeze the antibiotic ointment into it.

STOMACH UPSET

Occasionally, all dogs experience an upset stomach. Maybe they ate too many treats one day, or picked up a bit of a bug at puppy class! Start your pet on a bland diet of boiled hamburger and rice or mutton and rice. Also, yogurt with active cultures is great for post-diarrhea treatment. Dogs can

Cuts and punctures must be kept clean until thoroughly healed to avoid infection.

Shar-Pei can develop an upset stomach from eating too many treats or a simple bacteria or virus.

successfully be treated for diarrhea with human over-the-counter medications, but ask your veterinarian's office first. Any illness extending more than two days or

associated with a high fever should be seen by the veterinarian immediately.

BATH

While Shar-Pei are not overly fond of water, by making bathing a regular occurrence you can get the job done! Any good dog shampoo can get your pet clean. Be sure to keep the water temperature warm (no outdoor bathing in winter!) and wash the face with a washcloth, keeping water from the ears.

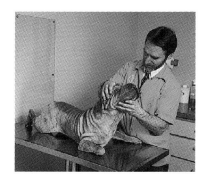

Not all veterinarians are specialists on all breeds of dogs, so it is important that the veterinarian you choose is up-to-date on illnesses that are specific to the Shar-Pei.

AMYLOIDOSIS

This is a complex illness that, very simply put, results in deposits on the kidney that eventually lead to kidney failure. (Amyloids are a sticky protein that can also build up on the liver and heart. It is similar to a disease called "Mediterranean fever" which is a human ailment found mainly in people of Semitic Mediterranean descent. It is hoped that the research being done on swollen hock syndrome and amyloidosis in Shar-Pei will benefit human science as well.) Some dogs exhibiting swollen hock syndrome eventually die from kidney failure associated with amyloidosis, but this is not definite. Make sure your veterinarian is up to date on the current research being done, and you will be in good hands.

Shar-Pei enjoy being groomed on a regular basis. Brushing on a weekly basis is all your pet will need—provided he stays out of the mud.

HEREDITARY DISEASES

As with all breeds of dogs, heredity of many illnesses is a factor that should not be overlooked. While there are no guarantees that the dog you choose (of any breed) will be healthy and problem free, your best defense is a good offense. Ask the breeder about the family history of your dog. Inquire regarding hip dysplasia (were the parents and grandparents OFA certified?), patellar luxation (slipping of the kneecaps), any known cases of amyloidosis in the dog's family, and the ages of the dog's parents and grandparents. If they have died, what were the causes? Does the breeder keep up with littermates, and if so, does he have any reports of any problems? No breeder can tell you that all of his dogs are perfectly healthy or that they have never had any problems. That is unrealistic in any breed! The more knowledgeable the breeder, the more informed you will be. A good breeder can tell you how likely you are to have a problem, but can not promise that you will not have a problem. They will, however, usually have a written contract that covers these areas, especially if you

Many breeders have their stock screened against the major hereditary diseases such as hip dysplasia, von Willebrand's disease and cataracts.

The family history of your dog is a good indication of what the future will bring. While this will not guarantee that the Shar-Pei you choose will be problem free, it is your best start.

are buying a show/breeding dog.

All breeds of dogs, including mixed breeds, are prone to some diseases. For Chinese Shar-Pei, the most common causes of death seem to be kidney failure or cancer. Occasionally we will see more unusual causes, as is the case with all dogs. Your best protection against both common and uncommon problems is good research before you buy, good veterinary care, and good consistent maintenance on your part. There are no guarantees with a dog's health, as with your own health. However, you can't stop living your life because you may someday be ill, nor should you stop yourself from owning a loving companion because the dog might get ill. Learn, study, and work with a breeder you trust, and then take good care of your package of wrinkled love!

SPORT of Purebred Dogs

Welcome to the exciting and sometimes frustrating sport of dogs. No doubt you are trying to learn more about dogs or you wouldn't be deep into this book. This section covers the basics that may entice you, further your knowledge and help you to understand the dog world. If you decide to give showing, obedience or any other dog activities a try, then I suggest you seek further help from the appropriate source.

Dog showing has been a very popular sport for a long time and has been taken quite seriously by some. Others only enjoy it as a hobby.

The Kennel Club in England was formed in 1859, the American Kennel Club was established in 1884 and the Canadian Kennel Club was formed in 1888. The purpose of these clubs was to register purebred dogs and maintain their Stud Books. In the beginning, the concept of registering dogs was not readily accepted. More than 36 million dogs have been enrolled in the AKC Stud Book since its inception in 1888. Presently the kennel clubs not only register dogs but adopt and enforce rules and regulations governing dog shows, obedience trials and field trials. Over the years they have fostered and encouraged interest in the health and welfare of the purebred dog. They routinely donate funds to veterinary research for study on genetic disorders.

The following are the addresses of the kennel clubs in the United States, Great Britain and Canada.

It takes time for both dog and handler to learn the routine of conformation showing. The point to keep in mind when moving the dog for the judge is to present the dog to his best.

The American Kennel Club
51 Madison Avenue
New York, NY 10010
(Their registry is located at: 5580 Centerview Drive, STE 200, Raleigh, NC 27606-3390)

The Kennel Club
1 Clarges Street
Piccadilly, London, WIY 8AB, England

The Canadian Kennel Club
111 Eglinton Avenue
East Toronto, Ontario M6S 4V7
Canada

Today there are numerous activities that are enjoyable for both the dog and the handler. Some of the activities include conformation showing, obedience competition, tracking, agility, the Canine Good Citizen Certificate, and a wide range of instinct tests that vary from breed to breed. Where you start depends upon your goals which early on may not be readily apparent.

PUPPY KINDERGARTEN

Every puppy will benefit from this class. PKT is the foundation for all future dog activities from conformation to "couch potatoes." Pet owners should make an effort to attend even if they never expect to show their dog. The class is designed for puppies about three months of age with graduation at approximately five months of age. All the puppies will be in the same age group and, even though some may be a little unruly, there should not be any real problem. This class will teach the puppy some beginning obedience. As in all obedience classes the owner learns how to train his own dog. The PKT class gives the puppy the opportunity to interact with other puppies in the same age group and exposes him to strangers, which is very important. Some dogs grow up with behavior problems, one of them being fear of strangers. As you can see, there can be much to gain from this class.

There are some basic obedience exercises that every dog should learn. Some of these can be started with puppy kindergarten.

Sit

One way of teaching the sit is to have your dog on your left side with the leash in your right hand, close to the collar. Pull up on the leash and at the same time reach around his hindlegs with your left hand and tuck them in. As you are doing this say, "Beau, sit." Always use the dog's name when you give an active command. Some owners like to use a treat holding it over the dog's head. The dog will need to sit to get the treat. Encourage the dog to hold the sit for a few seconds, which will eventually be the beginning of the Sit/Stay. Depending on how cooperative he is, you can rub him under the chin or stroke his back. It is a good time to establish eye contact.

Puppy Kindergarten Training will teach your Shar-Pei puppy some beginning obedience and teach you how to train your own dog.

Down

Sit the dog on your left side and kneel down beside him with the leash in your right hand. Reach over him with your left hand and grasp his left foreleg. With your right hand, take his right foreleg and pull his legs forward while you say, "Beau, down." If he tries to get up, lean on his shoulder to encourage him to stay down. It will relax your dog if you stroke his back while he is down. Try to encourage him to stay down for a few seconds as preparation for the Down/Stay.

Heel

The definition of heeling is the dog walking under control at your left heel. Your puppy will learn controlled walking in the puppy kindergarten class, which will eventually lead to heeling. The command is "Beau, heel," and you start off briskly with your left foot. Your leash is in your right hand and your left hand is holding it about half way down. Your left hand should be able to control the leash and there should be a little slack in it. You want him to walk with you with your leg somewhere between his nose and his shoulder. You need to encourage him to stay with you, not forging (in front of you) or lagging behind you. It is best to keep him on a fairly short lead. Do not allow the lead to become tight. It is far better to give him a little jerk when necessary and remind him to heel. When you come to a halt, be prepared physically to make him sit. It takes practice to become coordinated. There are excellent books on training that you may wish to purchase. Your instructor should be able to recommend one for you.

Always use a happy tone of voice when you call your Shar-Pei to you. Under no circumstances should you ever scold your dog after he has come to you.

Recall

This quite possibly is the most important exercise you will ever teach. It should be a pleasant experience. The puppy may learn to do random recalls while being attached to a long line such as a clothes line. Later the exercise will start with the dog sitting and staying until called. The command is "Beau, come." Let your command be happy. You want your dog to come willingly and faithfully. The recall could save his life if he sneaks out the door. In practicing the recall, let him jump on you or touch you before you reach for him. If he is shy, then kneel down to his level. Reaching for the insecure dog could frighten him, and he may not be willing to come again in the future. Lots of praise and a treat would be in order whenever you do a recall. Under no circumstances should you ever correct your dog when he has come to you. Later in formal obedience your dog will be required to sit in front of you after recalling and then go to heel position.

102

Conformation showing is our oldest dog sport. It is based on the dog's appearance–his structure, movement, and attitude.

CONFORMATION

Conformation showing is our oldest dog show sport. This type of showing is based on the dog's appearance–that is his structure, movement and attitude. When considering this type of showing, you need to be aware of your breed's standard and be able to evaluate your dog compared to that standard. The breeder of your puppy or other experienced breeders would be good sources for such an evaluation. Puppies can go through lots of changes over a period of time. I always say most puppies start out as promising hopefuls and then after maturing may be disappointing as show candidates. Even so this should not deter them from being excellent pets.

Usually conformation training classes are offered by the local

Conformation showing allows an owner and/ or handler to see how well their dog matches up to the standard. kennel or obedience clubs. These are excellent places for training puppies. The puppy should be able to walk on a lead before entering such a class. Proper ring procedure and technique for posing (stacking) the dog will be demonstrated as well as gaiting the dog. Usually certain patterns are used in the ring such as the triangle or the "L." Conformation class, like the PKT class, will give your youngster the opportunity to socialize with different breeds of dogs and humans too.

It takes some time to learn the routine of conformation showing. Usually one starts at the puppy matches which may be AKC Sanctioned or Fun Matches. These matches are generally for puppies from two or three months to a year old, and there may be classes for the adult over the age of 12 months. Similar to point shows, the classes are divided by sex and after completion of the classes in that breed or variety, the class winners compete for Best of Breed or Variety. The winner goes on to compete in the Group and the Group winners compete for Best in Match. No championship points are awarded for match wins.

A few matches can be great training for puppies even though there is no intention to go on showing. Matches enable the puppy to meet new people and be handled by a stranger—the judge. It is also a change of environment, which broadens the horizon for both dog and handler. Matches and other dog activities boost the confidence of the handler and especially the younger handlers.

This is Kasu's Pop The Cork with the author winning Reserve Winners Bitch. This award does not carry any points unless the Winners win is disallowed by the AKC.

Earning an AKC championship is built on a point system, which is different from Great Britain. To become an AKC Champion of Record the dog must earn 15 points. The number of points earned each time depends upon the number of dogs in competition. The number of points available at each show depends upon the breed, its sex and the location of the show. The United States is divided into ten AKC zones. Each zone has its own set of points. The purpose of the zones is to try to equalize the points available from breed to breed and area to area.The AKC adjusts the point scale annually.

The number of points that can be won at a show are between one and five. Three-, four- and five-point wins are considered majors. Not only does the dog need 15 points won under three different judges, but those points must include two majors under two different judges. Canada also works on a point system but majors are not required.

Dogs always show before bitches. The classes available to those seeking points are: Puppy (which may be divided into 6 to 9 months and 9 to 12 months); 12 to 18 months; Novice; Bred-by-Exhibitor; American-bred; and Open. The class winners of the same sex of each breed or variety compete against each other for Winners Dog and Winners Bitch. A Reserve Winners Dog and Reserve Winners Bitch are also awarded but do not carry any points unless the Winners win is disallowed by AKC. The Winners Dog and Bitch compete with the specials (those dogs that have attained championship) for Best of Breed or Variety, Best of Winners and Best of Opposite Sex. It is possible to pick up an extra point or even a major if the points are higher for the defeated winner than those of Best of Winners. The latter would get the higher total from the defeated winner.

Both handler and dog are expected to conduct themselves in a gentlemanly fashion in the ring, showing courtesy not only to the judge but to the other competitors as well.

Best of Breed is the top breed award, and at a specialty show, this is the highest of all awards. This is Ch. Acapella Xiao Peng's Lil Hobo winning a national specialty.

At an all-breed show, each Best of Breed or Variety winner will go on to his respective Group and then the Group winners will compete against each other for Best in Show. There are seven Groups: Sporting, Hounds, Working, Terriers, Toys, Non-Sporting and Herding. Obviously there are no Groups at speciality shows (those shows that have only one breed or a show such as the American Spaniel Club's Flushing Spaniel Show, which is for all flushing spaniel breeds).

Earning a championship in England is somewhat different since they do not have a point system. Challenge Certificates are awarded if the judge feels the dog is deserving regardless of the number of dogs in competition. A dog must earn three Challenge Certificates under three different judges, with at least one of these Certificates being won after the age of 12 months. Competition is very strong and entries may be higher than they are in the U.S. The Kennel Club's Challenge Certificates are only available at Championship Shows.

In England, The Kennel Club regulations require that certain dogs, Border Collies and Gundog breeds, qualify in a working capacity (i.e., obedience or field trials) before becoming a full Champion. If they do not qualify in the working aspect, then they are designated a Show Champion, which is equivalent to the AKC's Champion of Record. A Gundog may be granted the title of Field Trial Champion (FT Ch.) if it passes all the tests in the field but would also have to qualify in conformation before becoming a full Champion. A Border Collie that earns the title of Obedience Champion (Ob Ch.) must also qualify in the conformation ring before becoming a Champion.

The U.S. doesn't have a designation full Champion but does award for Dual and Triple Champions. The Dual Champion must be a Champion of Record, and either Champion Tracker, Herding Champion, Obedience Trial Champion or Field Champion. Any dog that has been awarded the titles of Champion of Record, and any two of the following: Champion Tracker, Herding Champion, Obedience Trial Champion or Field Champion, may be designated as a Triple Champion.

The shows in England seem to put more emphasis on breeder judges than those in the U.S. There is much competition within the breeds. Therefore the quality of the individual breeds should be very good. In the United States we tend to have more "all around judges" (those that judge multiple breeds) and use the breeder judges at the specialty shows. Breeder judges are more familiar with their own breed since they are actively breeding that breed or did so at one time. Americans emphasize Group and Best in Show wins and promote them accordingly.

It is my understanding that the shows in England can be very large and extend over several days, with the Groups being scheduled on

The Westminster Kennel Club Dog Show is the most prestigious in the United States. It is held in New York City annually and is the oldest show in the world.

This is Tainan's Tootsie of Chu'Hill winning Best of Opposite Sex in Sweepstakes.

different days. I believe there is only one all-breed show in the U.S. that extends over two days, the Westminster Kennel Club Show. In our country we have cluster shows, where several different clubs will use the same show site over consecutive days.

Westminster Kennel Club is our most prestigious show although the entry is limited to 2500. In recent years, entry has been limited to Champions. This show is more formal than the majority of the shows with the judges wearing formal attire and the handlers fashionably dressed. In most instances the quality of the dogs is superb. After all, it is a show of Champions. It is a good show to study the AKC registered breeds and is by far the most exciting—especially since it is televised! WKC is one of the few shows in this country that is still benched. This means the dog must be in his benched area during the show hours except when he is being groomed, in the ring, or being exercised.

Typically, the handlers are very particular about their appearances. They are careful not to wear something that will detract from their dog but will perhaps enhance it. American ring procedure is quite formal compared to that of other countries. I remember being reprimanded by a judge because I made a suggestion to a friend holding my second dog outside the ring. I certainly could have used more discretion so I would not call attention to myself. There is a certain etiquette expected between the judge and exhibitor and among the other exhibitors. Of course it is not always the case but the judge is supposed to be polite, not engaging in small talk or even acknowledging that he knows the handler. I understand that there is a more informal and relaxed atmosphere at the shows in other countries. For instance, the dress code is more casual. I can see where this might be more fun for the exhibitor and especially for the novice.

Mo-Ti Chops Beaux-Art handled by Barbara Dion winning BOS at a specialty show.

This country is very handler-oriented in many of the breeds. It is true, in most instances, that the experienced professional handler can present the dog better and will have a feel for what a judge likes.

In England, Crufts is The Kennel Club's own show and is most assuredly the largest dog show in the world. They've been known to have an entry of nearly 20,000, and the show lasts four days. Entry is only gained by qualifying through winning in specified classes at another Championship Show. Westminster is strictly conformation, but Crufts exhibitors and spectators enjoy not only conformation but obedience, agility and a multitude of exhibitions as well. Obedience was admitted in 1957 and agility in 1983.

If you are handling your own dog, please give some consideration to your apparel. For sure the dress code at matches is more informal than the point shows. However, you should wear something a

Crufts Dog Show is England's most important show. Handlers and their dogs have a large competition field, nearly 20,000 dogs are entered over four days of showing.

little more appropriate than beach attire or ragged jeans and bare feet. If you check out the handlers and see what is presently fashionable, you'll catch on. Men usually dress with a shirt and tie and a nice sports coat. Whether you are male or female, you will want to wear comfortable clothes and shoes. You need to be able to run with your dog and you certainly don't want to take a chance of falling and hurting yourself. Heaven forbid, if nothing else, you'll upset your dog. Women usually wear a dress or two-piece outfit, preferably with pockets to carry bait, comb, brush, etc. In this case men are the lucky ones with all their pockets. Ladies, think about where your dress will be if you need to kneel on the floor and also think about running. Does it allow freedom to do so?

Years ago, after toting around all the baby paraphernalia, I found toting the dog and necessities a breeze. You need to take along dog; crate; ex pen (if you use one); extra newspaper; water pail and water; all required grooming equipment, including hair dryer and extension cord; table; chair for you; bait for dog and lunch for you and friends; and, last but not least, clean up materials, such as plastic bags, paper towels, and perhaps a bath towel and some shampoo—just in case. Don't forget your entry confirmation and directions to the show.

If you are showing in obedience, then you will want to wear pants. Many of our top obedience handlers wear pants that are color-coordinated with their dogs. The philosophy is that imperfections in the black dog will be less obvious next to your black pants.

Whether you are showing in conformation, Junior Showmanship or obedience, you need to watch the clock and be sure you are not late. It is customary to pick up your conformation armband a few minutes before the start of the class. They will not wait for you and if you are on the show grounds and not in the ring, you will upset everyone. It's a little more complicated picking up your obedience armband if you show later in the class. If you have not picked up your armband and they get to your number, you may not be allowed to show. It's best to pick up your armband early, but then you may show earlier than expected if other handlers don't pick up. Customarily all conflicts should be discussed with the judge prior to the start of the class.

Junior Showmanship

The Junior Showmanship Class is a wonderful way to build self confidence even if there are no aspirations of staying with the dog-show game later in life. Frequently, Junior Showmanship becomes the background of those who become successful exhibitors/handlers in the future. In some instances it is taken very seriously, and success is measured in terms of wins. The Junior Handler is judged solely on his ability and skill in presenting his dog. The dog's conformation is not to be considered by the judge. Even so the condition and grooming of the dog may be a reflection upon the handler.

Usually the matches and point shows include different classes. The Junior Handler's dog may be entered in a breed or obedience class and even shown by another person in that class. Junior Showmanship classes are usually divided by age and perhaps sex. The age is determined by the handler's age on the day of the show. The classes are:

In Junior Showmanship competition, children between the ages of ten and seventeen handle dogs owned by their immediate families. Ch. Show Me's Royal Flush handled by Malinda Bulgin.

113

Novice Junior for those at least ten and under 14 years of age who at time of entry closing have not won three first places in a Novice Class at a licensed or member show.

Novice Senior for those at least 14 and under 18 years of age who at the time of entry closing have not won three first places in a Novice Class at a licensed or member show.

Open Junior for those at least ten and under 14 years of age who at the time of entry closing have won at least three first places in a Novice Junior Showmanship Class at a licensed or member show with competition present.

Open Senior for those at least 14 and under 18 years of age who at time of entry closing have won at least three first places in a Novice Junior Showmanship Class at a licensed or member show with competition present.

Junior Handlers must include their AKC Junior Handler number on each show entry. This needs to be obtained from the AKC.

CANINE GOOD CITIZEN

The AKC sponsors a program to encourage dog owners to train their dogs. Local clubs perform the pass/fail tests, and dogs who pass are awarded a Canine Good Citizen Certificate. Proof of vaccination is required at the time of participation. The test includes:

1. Accepting a friendly stranger.
2. Sitting politely for petting.
3. Appearance and grooming.
4. Walking on a loose leash.

Accepting a Nylafloss® from this friendly little boy is one way this Shar-Pei pup is learning his socialization skills.

5. Walking through a crowd.
6. Sit and down on command/staying in place.
7. Come when called.
8. Reaction to another dog.
9. Reactions to distractions.
10. Supervised separation.

A positive reaction to another dog is one of the exercises that must be completed to earn a Canine Good Citizen Certificate.

If more effort was made by pet owners to accomplish these exercises, fewer dogs would be cast off to the humane shelter.

OBEDIENCE

Leash training is probably the most important thing you can teach your Shar-Pei. These pups are anxious to get their lesson going.

Obedience is necessary, without a doubt, but it can also become a wonderful hobby or even an obsession. In my opinion, obedience classes and competition can provide wonderful companionship, not only

with your dog but with your classmates or fellow competitors. It is always gratifying to discuss your dog's problems with others who have had similar experiences. The AKC acknowledged Obedience around 1936, and it has changed tremendously even though many of the exercises are basically the same. Today, obedience competition is just that—very competitive. Even so, it is possible for every obedience exhibitor to come home a winner (by earning qualifying scores) even though he/she may not earn a placement in the class.

Part of earning an obedience title is the long sit. To earn a CD, your Shar-Pei must sit for one minute off leash, and to earn a CDX, he must sit for three minutes.

Most of the obedience titles are awarded after earning three qualifying scores (legs) in the appropriate class under three different judges. These classes offer a perfect score of 200, which is extremely rare. Each of the class exercises has its own point value. A leg is earned after receiving a score of at least 170 and at least 50 percent of the points available in each exercise. The titles are:

Companion Dog—CD
This is called the Novice Class and the exercises are:

1. Heel on leash and figure 8	40 points
2. Stand for examination	30 points
3. Heel free	40 points
4. Recall	30 points
5. Long sit—one minute	30 points
6. Long down—three minutes	30 points
Maximum total score	200 points

Companion Dog Excellent—CDX
This is the Open Class and the exercises are:

1. Heel off leash and figure 8	40 points
2. Drop on recall	30 points
3. Retrieve on flat	20 points
4. Retrieve over high jump	30 points
5. Broad jump	20 points
6. Long sit—three minutes (out of sight)	30 points
7. Long down—five minutes (out of sight)	30 points
Maximum total score	200 points

Utility Dog—UD

The Utility Class exercises are:

1. Signal Exercise	40 points
2. Scent discrimination-Article 1	30 points
3. Scent discrimination-Article 2	30 points
4. Directed retrieve	30 points
5. Moving stand and examination	30 points
6. Directed jumping	40 points
Maximum total score	200 points

After achieving the UD title, you may feel inclined to go after the UDX and/or OTCh. The UDX (Utility Dog Excellent) title went into effect in January 1994. It is not easily attained. The title requires qualifying simultaneously ten times in Open B and Utility B but not necessarily at consecutive shows.

The OTCh (Obedience Trial Champion) is awarded after the dog has earned his UD and then goes on to earn 100 championship points, a first place in Utility, a first place in Open and another first place in either class. The placements must be won under three different judges at all-breed obedience trials. The points are determined by the number of dogs competing in the Open B and Utility B classes. The OTCh title precedes the dog's name.

Obedience matches (AKC Sanctioned, Fun, and Show and Go) are usually available. Usually they are sponsored by the local obedience clubs. When preparing an obedience dog for a title, you will find matches very helpful. Fun Matches and Show and Go Matches are more lenient in allowing you to

This Shar-Pei competes in agility, a competition which can be described as an obstacle course for dogs to test their speed, coordination and intelligence.

make corrections in the ring. I frequently train (correct) in the ring and inform the judge that I would like to do so and to please mark me "exhibition." This means that I will not be eligible for any prize. This type of training is usually very necessary for the Open and Utility Classes. AKC Sanctioned Obedience Matches do not allow corrections in the ring since they must abide by the AKC Obedience Regulations. If

Executing the bar jump at an agility competition.

you are interested in showing in obedience, then you should contact the AKC for a copy of the Obedience Regulations.

AGILITY

Agility was first introduced by John Varley in England at the Crufts Dog Show, February 1978, but Peter Meanwell, competitor and judge, actually developed the idea. It was officially recognized in the early '80s. Agility is extremely popular in England and Canada and growing in popularity in the U.S. The AKC acknowledged agility in August 1994. Dogs must be at least 12 months of age to be entered. It is a fascinating sport that the dog, handler and spectators enjoy to the utmost. Agility is a spectator sport! The dog performs off lead. The handler either runs with his dog or positions himself on the course and directs his dog with verbal and hand signals over a timed course over or through a variety of obstacles including a time out or pause. One of the main drawbacks to agility is finding a place to train. The obstacles take up a lot of space and it is very time consuming to put up and take down courses.

The titles earned at AKC agility trials are Novice Agility Dog (NAD), Open Agility Dog (OAD), Agility Dog Excellent (ADX), and Master Agility Excellent (MAX). In order to acquire an agility title, a dog must earn a qualifying score in its respective class on three separate occasions under two different judges. The MAX will be awarded after earning ten qualifying scores in the Agility Excellent Class.

General Information

Obedience, tracking and agility allow the purebred dog with an Indefinite Listing Privilege (ILP) number or a limited registration to be exhibited and earn titles. Application must be made to the AKC for an ILP number.

The American Kennel Club publishes a monthly *Events* magazine that is part of the *Gazette*, their official journal for the sport of purebred dogs. The *Events* section lists upcoming shows and the secretary or superintendent for them. The majority of the conformation shows in the U.S. are overseen by licensed superintendents. Generally the entry closing date is approximately two-and-a-half weeks before the actual show. Point shows are fairly expensive, while the match shows cost about one third of the point show entry fee. Match shows usually take entries the day of the show but some are pre-entry. The best way to find match show information is through your local kennel club. Upon asking, the

Ch. Linns Ping CD is the first dog in the Chinese Shar-Pei Club of America registry to earn an obedience title and a conformation title.

AKC can provide you with a list of superintendents, and you can write and ask to be put on their mailing lists.

Obedience trial and tracking test information is available through the AKC. Frequently these events are not superintended, but put on by the host club. Therefore you would make the entry with the event's secretary.

As you have read, there are numerous activities you can share with your dog. Regardless what you do, it does take

Agility is a fascinating sport enjoyed by dog, handler and spectators alike. Shar-Pei have proven exceptional in most areas of agility

teamwork. Your dog can only benefit from your attention and training. I hope this chapter has enlightened you and hope, if nothing else, you will attend a show here and there. Perhaps you will start with a puppy kindergarten class, and who knows where it may lead!

DENTAL CARE for Your Dog's Life

So you've got a new puppy! You also have a new set of puppy teeth in your household. Anyone who has ever raised a puppy is abundantly aware of these new teeth. Your puppy will chew anything it can reach, chase your shoelaces, and play "tear the rag" with any piece of clothing it can find. When puppies are newly born, they have no teeth. At about four weeks of age, puppies of most breeds begin to develop their deciduous or baby teeth. They begin eating semi-solid food, fighting and biting with their litter mates, and learning discipline from their mother. As their new teeth come in, they inflict more pain on their mother's breasts, so her feeding sessions become less frequent and shorter. By six or eight weeks, the mother will start growling to warn her pups when they are fighting too roughly or hurting her as they nurse too much with their new teeth.

Puppies need to chew. It is a necessary part of their physical and mental development. They develop muscles and necessary life skills as they drag objects around, fight over possession, and vocalize alerts and warnings. Puppies chew on things to explore their world. They are using their sense of taste to determine what is food and what is not. How else can they tell an electrical cord from a lizard? At about four months of age, most puppies begin shedding their baby teeth. Often these

All puppies love to chew, and Shar-Pei are no exception to this. Gumabone® products, due to their softer composition, are excellent chew toys for puppies and less powerful chewers.

teeth need some help to come out and make way for the permanent teeth. The incisors (front teeth) will be replaced first. Then, the adult canine or fang teeth erupt. When the baby tooth is not shed before the permanent tooth comes in, veterinarians call it a retained deciduous tooth. This condition will often cause gum infections by trapping hair and debris between the permanent tooth and the retained baby tooth.

A chicken-flavored Gumabone® has tiny particles of chicken powder embedded in it to keep your Shar-Pei interested.

Nylafloss® is an excellent device for puppies to use. They can toss it, drag it, and chew on the many surfaces it presents. The baby teeth can catch in the nylon material, aiding in their removal. Puppies that have adequate chew toys will have less destructive behavior, develop more

Molded rawhide, called Roar-Hide™, is very hard and safe for your dog. It is eagerly accepted by most dogs including Shar-Pei.

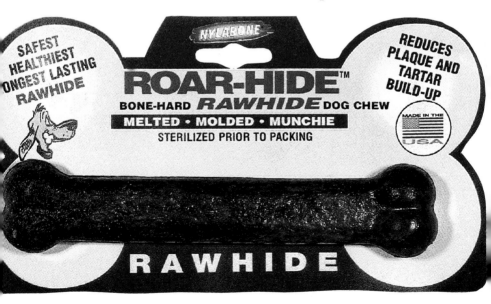

physically, and have less chance of retained deciduous teeth.

During the first year, your dog should be seen by your veterinarian at regular intervals. Your veterinarian will let you know when to bring in your puppy for vaccinations and parasite examinations. At each visit, your veterinarian should inspect the lips, teeth, and mouth as part of a complete physical examination. You should take some part in the maintenance of your dog's oral health. You should examine your dog's mouth weekly throughout his first year to make sure there are no sores, foreign objects, tooth problems, etc. If your dog drools excessively, shakes its head, or has bad breath, consult your veterinarian. By the time your dog is six months old, the permanent teeth are all in and plaque can start to accumulate on the tooth surfaces. This is when your dog needs to develop good dental-care habits to prevent calculus build-up on its teeth. Brushing is best. That is a fact that cannot be denied. However, some

You should examine your Shar-Pei's mouth weekly for the first year of its life to make sure there are no sores, foreign objects, tooth problems, etc.

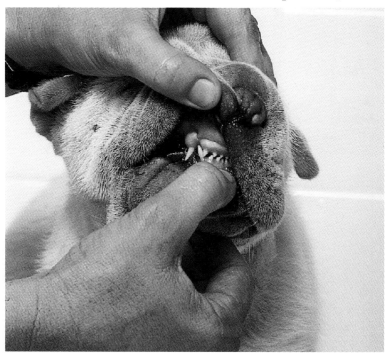

dogs do not like their teeth brushed regularly, or you may not be able to accomplish the task. In that case, you should consider a product that will help prevent plaque and calculus build-up.

The Plaque Attackers® and Galileo Bone® are other excellent choices for the first three years of a dog's life. Their shapes make them interesting for the dog. As the dog chews on them, the solid polyurethane massages the gums which improves the blood circulation to the periodontal tissues. Projections on the chew devices increase the surface and are in contact with the tooth for more efficient cleaning. The unique shape and consistency prevent your dog from exerting excessive force on his own teeth or from breaking off pieces of the bone. If your dog is an aggressive chewer or weighs more than 55 pounds (25 kg), you should consider giving him a Nylabone®, the most durable chew product on the market.

The Nylafloss® and the Gumabone® Frisbee® * are excellent chew devices for your Shar-Pei puppy. *The trademark Frisbee is used under license from Mattel, Inc., California, USA.

The Gumabones®, made by the Nylabone Company, is constructed of strong polyurethane, which is softer than nylon. Less powerful chewers prefer the Gumabones® to the Nylabones®. A super option for your dog is the Hercules Bone®, a uniquely shaped bone named after the great Olympian for its exception strength. Like all Nylabone products, they are specially scented to make them attractive to your dog. Ask your veterinarian about these bones and he will validate the good doctor's prescription: Nylabones® not only give your dog a good chewing workout but also help to save your dog's teeth (and even his life, as it protects him from possible fatal periodontal diseases).

By the time dogs are four years old, 75% of them have periodontal disease. It is the most common infection in dogs. Yearly examinations by your veterinarian are essential to maintaining your dog's good health. If your veterinarian detects periodontal disease, he or she may recommend a prophylactic cleaning. To do a thorough cleaning, it will be necessary to put your dog under anesthesia. With modern gas anesthetics and monitoring equipment, the procedure is pretty safe. Your veterinarian will scale the teeth with an ultrasound scaler or hand instrument. This removes the calculus from the teeth. If there are calculus deposits below the gum line, the veterinarian will plane the roots to make them smooth. After all of the calculus has been removed, the teeth are polished with pumice in a polishing cup. If any medical or surgical treatment is needed, it is done at this time. The final step would be fluoride treatment and your follow-up treatment at home. If the periodontal disease is advanced, the veterinarian may prescribe a medicated mouth rinse or antibiotics for use at home. Make sure your dog has safe, clean and attractive chew toys and treats. Chooz® treats are another way of using a consumable treat to help keep your dog's teeth clean.

Rawhide is the most popular of all materials for a dog to chew. This has never been good news to dog owners, because rawhide is inherently very dangerous for dogs. Thousands of dogs have died from rawhide, having swallowed the hide after it has become soft and mushy, only to cause stomach and intestinal blockage. A new rawhide product on the market has finally solved the problem of rawhide: molded Roar-Hide® from Nylabone. These are composed of processed, cut up, and melted American rawhide injected into your dog's favorite shape: a dog bone. These dog-safe devices smell and taste like rawhide but don't break up. The ridges on the bones help to fight tartar build-up on the teeth and they last ten times longer than the usual rawhide chews.

As your dog ages, professional examination and cleaning

should become more frequent. The mouth

Nylabone® products are so much fun for your Shar-Pei that he will never want to put them down. These devices are therapeutic and help promote cleaner teeth and gums and better breath too.

Nylafloss® is made of nylon rope which acts as a dental floss and does not rot like cotton.

should be inspected at least once a year. Your veterinarian may recommend visits every six months. In the geriatric patient, organs such as the heart, liver, and kidneys do not function as well as when they were young. Your veterinarian will probably want to test these organs' functions prior to using general anesthesia for dental cleaning. If your dog is a good chewer and you work closely with your veterinarian, your dog can keep all of its teeth all of its life. However, as your dog ages, his sense of smell, sight, and taste will diminish. He may not have the desire to chase, trap or chew his toys. He will also not have the energy to chew for long periods, as arthritis and periodontal disease make chewing painful. This will leave you with more responsibility for keeping his teeth clean and healthy. The dog that would not let you brush his teeth at one year of age, may let you brush his teeth now that he is ten years old.

If you train your dog with good chewing habits as a puppy, he will have healthier teeth throughout his life.

IDENTIFICATION and Finding the Lost Dog

There are several ways of identifying your dog. The old standby is a collar with dog license, rabies, and ID tags. Unfortunately collars have a way of being separated from the dog and tags fall off. I am not suggesting you shouldn't use a collar and tags. If they stay intact and on the dog, they are the quickest way of identification.

For several years owners have been tattooing their dogs. Some tattoos use a number with a registry. Here lies the problem because there are several registries to check. If you wish to tattoo, use your social security number. The humane shelters have the means to trace it. It is usually done on the inside of the rear thigh. The area is first shaved and numbed. There is no pain, although a few dogs do not like the buzzing sound. Occasionally tattooing is not legible and needs to be redone.

An identification tag can be attached to your Shar-Pei's collar. This should be complete with an address and phone number so that your dog can be returned to you should he be lost.

The newest method of identification is microchipping. The microchip is a computer chip that is no larger than a grain of rice. The veterinarian implants it by injection between the shoulder blades. The dog feels no discomfort. If your dog is lost and picked up by the humane society, they can trace you by scanning the microchip, which has its own code. Microchip scanners are friendly to other brands of microchips and their registries. The microchip comes with a dog tag saying the dog is microchipped. It is the safest way of identifying your dog.

FINDING THE LOST DOG

I am sure you will agree with me that there would be little worse than losing your dog. Responsible pet owners rarely lose their dogs. They do not let their dogs run free because they don't want harm to come to them. Not only that but in most, if not all, states there is a leash law.

Beware of fenced-in yards. They can be a hazard. Dogs find ways to escape either over or under the fence. Another fast

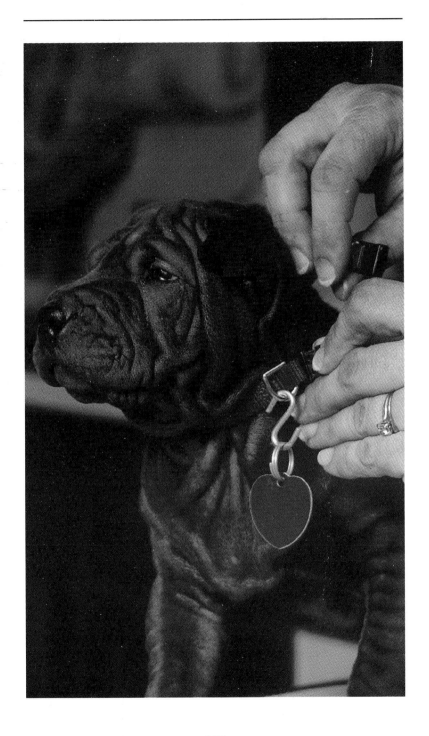

exit is through the gate that perhaps the neighbor's child left unlocked.

Below is a list that hopefully will be of help to you if you need it. Remember don't give up, keep looking. Your dog is worth your efforts.

1. Contact your neighbors and put flyers with a photo on it in their mailboxes. Information you should include would be the dog's name, breed, sex, color, age, source of identification, when your dog was last seen and where, and your name and phone numbers. It may be helpful to say the dog needs medical care. Offer a *reward*.

A recent method of identification is microchipping. The microchip is actually a computer chip that is no bigger than a grain of rice which is inserted under the dog's skin.

2. Check all local shelters daily. It is also possible for your dog to be picked up away from home and end up in an out-of-the-way shelter.

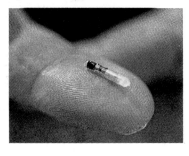

Check these too. Go in person. It is not good enough to call. Most shelters are limited on the time they can hold dogs then they are put up for adoption or euthanized. There is the possibility that your dog will not make it to the shelter for several days. Your dog could have been wandering or someone may have tried to keep him.

3. Notify all local veterinarians. Call and send flyers.
4. Call your breeder. Frequently breeders are contacted when one of their breed is found.
5. Contact the rescue group for your breed.
6. Contact local schools—children may have seen your dog.
7. Post flyers at the schools, groceries, gas stations, convenience stores, veterinary clinics, groomers and any other place that will allow them.
8. Advertise in the newspaper.
9. Advertise on the radio.

A lost dog will be very frightened and will try to hide in a most inconspicuous spot. This Shar-Pei seems to be hiding behind the trunk of a tree.

TRAVELING with Your Dog

The earlier you start traveling with your new puppy or dog, the better. He needs to become accustomed to traveling. However, some dogs are nervous riders and become carsick easily. It is helpful if he starts with an empty stomach. Do not despair, as it will go better if you continue taking him with you on short fun rides. How would you feel if every time you rode in the car you stopped at the doctor's for an injection? You would soon dread that nasty car. Older dogs that tend to get carsick may have more of a problem adjusting to traveling. Those dogs that are having a serious problem may benefit from some medication prescribed by the veterinarian.

Do give your dog a chance to relieve himself before getting into the car. It is a good idea to be prepared for a clean up with a leash, paper towels, bag and terry cloth towel.

The safest place for your dog is in a fiberglass crate, although close confinement can promote carsickness in some dogs. If your dog is nervous you can try letting him ride on the seat next to you or in someone's lap.

An alternative to the crate would be to use a car harness made for dogs and/or a safety strap attached to the harness or collar. Whatever you do, do not let your dog ride in the back of

Shar-Pei love to accompany their owners everywhere. This little wagon is not a safe means of travel and should be used only in play.

132

a pickup truck unless he is securely tied on a very short lead. I've seen trucks stop quickly and, even though the dog was tied, it fell out and was dragged.

I do occasionally let my dogs ride loose with me because I really enjoy their companionship, but in all honesty they are safer in their crates. I have a friend whose van rolled in an accident but his dogs, in their fiberglass crates, were not injured nor did they escape. Another advantage of the crate is that it is a safe place to leave him if you need to run into the store. Otherwise you wouldn't be able to leave the windows down. Keep in mind that while many dogs are overly protective in their crates, this may not be enough to deter dognappers. In some states it is

The Shar-Pei is a great traveling companion, but a basket does not make a good means of transport.

A dog crate is by far the safest means for your dog to travel. There are different models available from pet shops everywhere.

against the law to leave a dog in the car unattended.

Never leave a dog loose in the car wearing a collar and leash. I have known more than one dog that has killed himself by hanging. Do not let him put his head out an open window. Foreign debris can be blown into his eyes. When leaving your dog unattended in a car, consider the temperature. It can take less than five minutes to reach temperatures over 100 degrees Fahrenheit.

TRIPS

Perhaps you are taking a trip. Give consideration to what is best for your dog—traveling with you or boarding. When traveling by car, van or motor home, you need to think ahead about locking your vehicle. In all probability you have many valuables in the car and do not wish to leave it unlocked. Perhaps most valuable and not replaceable is your dog. Give thought to securing your vehicle and providing adequate ventilation for him. Another consideration for you when traveling with your dog is medical problems that may arise and little inconveniences, such as exposure to external parasites. Some areas of the country are quite flea infested. You may want to carry flea spray with you. This is even a good idea when staying in motels. Quite possibly you are not the only occupant of the room.

Unbelievably many motels and even hotels do allow canine guests, even some very first-class ones. Gaines Pet Foods Corporation publishes *Touring With Towser*, a directory of domestic hotels and motels that accommodate guests with dogs. Their address is Gaines TWT, PO Box 5700, Kankakee, IL, 60902. I would recommend you call ahead to any motel that you may be considering and see if they accept pets. Sometimes it is necessary to pay a deposit against room damage. Of course you are more likely to gain accommodations for a small dog than a large dog. Also the management feels reassured when you mention that your dog will be crated. Since my dogs tend to bark when I leave the room, I leave the TV on nearly full blast to deaden the noises outside that tend to encourage my dogs to bark. If you do travel with your dog, take along plenty of baggies so that you can clean up after him. When we all do our share in cleaning up, we make it possible for motels to continue accepting our pets. As a matter of fact, you should practice cleaning up everywhere you take your dog.

Depending on where your are traveling, you may need an up-to-date health certificate issued by your veterinarian. It is good policy to take along your dog's medical information, which would include the name, address and phone number of your veterinarian, vaccination record, rabies certificate, and any medication he is taking.

Air Travel

When traveling by air, you need to contact the airlines to check their policy. Usually you have to make arrangements up to a couple of weeks in advance for traveling with your dog. The airlines require your dog to travel in an airline approved fiberglass crate. Usually these can be purchased through the airlines but they are also readily available in most pet-supply stores. If your

Your Shar-Pei will enjoy all the comforts of home while you are away. Be sure to bring your pet's bed and any special toys he may have to make him as comfortable as possible.

dog is not accustomed to a crate, then it is a good idea to get him acclimated to it before your trip. The day of the actual trip you should withhold water about one hour ahead of departure and no food for about 12 hours. The airlines generally have temperature restrictions, which do not allow pets to travel if it is either too cold or too hot. Frequently these restrictions are based on the temperatures at the departure and arrival airports. It's best to inquire about a health certificate. These usually need to be issued within ten days of departure. You should arrange for non-stop, direct flights and if a commuter plane should be involved, check to see if it will carry dogs. Some don't. The Humane Society of the United States has put together a tip sheet for airline traveling. You can receive a copy by sending a self-addressed stamped envelope to:

The Humane Society of the United States
Tip Sheet
2100 L Street NW
Washington, DC 20037.

Regulations differ for traveling outside of the country and are sometimes changed without notice. Well in advance you need to write or call the appropriate consulate or agricultural department for instructions. Some countries have lengthy quarantines (six months), and countries differ in their rabies vaccination requirements. For instance, it may have to be given at least 30 days ahead of your departure.

Do make sure your dog is wearing proper identification. You never know when you might be in an accident and separated from your dog. Or your dog could be frightened and somehow manage to escape and run away. When I travel, my dogs wear collars with engraved nameplates with my name, phone number and city.

Another suggestion would be to carry in-case-of-emergency instructions. These would include the

Should your Shar-Pei become lost, an identification tag will let anyone who finds him return him to you promptly.

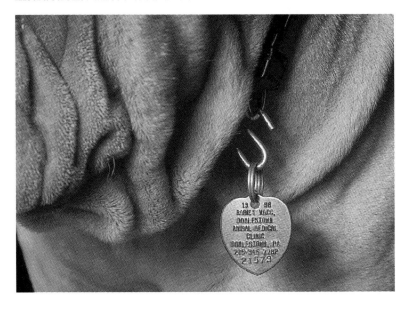

address and phone number of a relative or friend, your veterinarian's name, address and phone number, and your dog's medical information.

BOARDING KENNELS
Perhaps you have decided that you need to board your dog. Your veterinarian can recommend a good boarding facility or possibly a pet sitter that will come to your house. It is customary for the boarding kennel to ask for proof of vaccination for the DHLPP, rabies and bordetella vaccine. The bordetella should have been given within six months of boarding. This is for your protection. If they do not ask for this proof I would not board at their kennel. Ask about flea control. Those dogs that suffer flea-bite allergy can get in trouble at a boarding

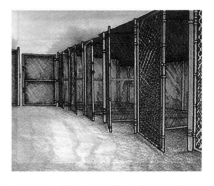

A reputable boarding kennel will require that dogs receive the vaccination for kennel cough no less than two weeks before their scheduled stay.

kennel. Unfortunately boarding kennels are limited on how much they are able to do.

For more information on pet sitting, contact NAPPS:
National Association of Professional Pet Sitters
1200 G Street, NW
Suite 760
Washington, DC 20005.

Our clinic has technicians that pet sit and technicians that board clinic patients in their homes. This may be an alternative for you. Ask your veterinarian if they have an employee that can help you. There is a definite advantage of having a technician care for your dog, especially if your dog is on medication or is a senior citizen.

You can write for a copy of *Traveling With Your Pet* from ASPCA, Education Department, 441 E. 92nd Street, New York, NY 10128.

BEHAVIOR and Canine Communication

Studies of the human/animal bond point out the importance of the unique relationships that exist between people and their pets. Those of us who share our lives with pets understand the special part they play through companionship, service and protection.

Senior citizens show more concern for their own eating habits when they have the responsibility of feeding a dog. Seeing that their dog is routinely exercised encourages the owner to think of schedules that otherwise may seem unimportant to the senior citizen. The older owner may be arthritic and feeling poorly but with responsibility for his dog he has a reason to get up and get moving. It is a big plus if his dog is an attention seeker who will demand such from his owner.

Well-bred Shar-Pei have excellent temperaments and are very agreeable dogs. They love all people, especially children.

Over the last couple of decades, it has been shown that pets relieve the stress of those who lead busy lives. Owning a pet has been known to lessen the occurrence of heart attack and stroke.

Many single folks thrive on the companionship of a dog. Lifestyles are very different from a long time ago, and today more individuals seek the single life. However, they receive fulfillment from owning a dog.

Most likely the majority of our dogs live in family environments. The companionship they provide is well worth the effort involved. In my opinion, every child should have the opportunity to have a family dog. Dogs teach responsibility through understanding their care, feelings and even respecting their life cycles. Frequently those children who have not been exposed to dogs grow up afraid of dogs, which isn't good. Dogs sense timidity and some will take advantage of the situation.

Today more dogs are serving as service dogs. Since the origination of the Seeing Eye dogs years ago, we now have

trained hearing dogs. Also dogs are trained to provide service for the handicapped and are able to perform many different tasks for their owners. Search and Rescue dogs, with their handlers, are sent throughout the world to assist in recovery of disaster victims. They are life savers.

Therapy dogs are very popular with nursing homes, and some hospitals even allow them to visit. The inhabitants truly look forward to their visits. I have taken a couple of my dogs visiting and left in tears when I saw the response of the patients. They wanted and were allowed to have my dogs in their beds to hold and love.

Nationally there is a Pet Awareness Week to educate students and others about the value and basic care of our pets. Many countries take an even greater interest in their pets than Americans do. In

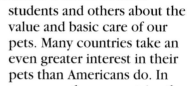

Shar-Pei make excellent therapy dogs. They are very popular with nursing homes and hospitals and visit these on a regular basis.

those countries the pets are allowed to accompany their owners into restaurants and shops, etc. In the U.S. this freedom is only available to our service dogs. Even so we think very highly of the human/animal bond.

CANINE BEHAVIOR

Canine behavior problems are the number-one reason for pet owners to dispose of their dogs, either through new homes, humane shelters or euthanasia. Unfortunately there are too many owners who are unwilling to devote the necessary time to properly train their dogs. On the other hand, there are those who not only are concerned about inherited health problems but are also aware of the dog's mental stability.

You may realize that a breed and his group relatives (i.e., sporting, hounds, etc.) show tendencies to behavioral characteristics. An experienced breeder can acquaint you with

This magnificent array of Shar-Pei quality, with their breeder Elly Paulus, represents Khan Du Kennels.

his breed's personality. Unfortunately many breeds are labeled with poor temperaments when actually the breed as a whole is not affected but only a small percentage of individuals within the breed.

If the breed in question is very popular, then of course there may be a higher number of unstable dogs. Do not label a breed good or bad. I know of absolutely awful-tempered dogs within one of our most popular, lovable breeds.

Inheritance and environment contribute to the dog's behavior. Some naïve people suggest inbreeding as the cause of bad temperaments. Inbreeding only results in poor behavior if the ancestors carry the trait. If there are excellent temperaments behind the dogs, then inbreeding will promote good temperaments in the offspring. Did you ever consider

Start socializing your Shar-Pei at an early age. It is very important that your puppy feels comfortable around people and other dogs.

that inbreeding is what sets the characteristics of a breed? A purebred dog is the end result of inbreeding. This does not spare the mixed-breed dog from the same problems. Mixed-breed dogs frequently are the offspring of purebred dogs.

When planning a breeding, I like to observe the potential stud and his offspring in the show ring. If I see unruly behavior, I try to look into it further. I want to know if it is genetic or environmental, due to the lack of training and socialization. A good breeder will avoid breeding mentally unsound dogs.

Not too many decades ago most of our dogs led a different lifestyle than what is prevalent today. Usually mom stayed home so the dog had human companionship and someone to discipline it if needed. Not much was expected from the dog. Today's mom works and everyone's life is at a much faster pace.

The dog may have to adjust to being a "weekend" dog. The family is gone all day during the week, and the dog is left to his own devices for entertainment. Some dogs sleep all day waiting for their family to come home and others become wigwam wreckers if given the opportunity. Crates do ensure the safety of the dog and the house. However, he could become a physically and emotionally cripple if he doesn't get enough exercise and attention. We still appreciate and want the companionship of our dogs although we expect more from them. In many cases we tend to forget dogs are just that—*dogs* not human beings.

I own several dogs who are left crated during the day but I do try to make time for them in the evenings and on the weekends. Also we try to do something together before I leave for work. Maybe it helps them to have the companionship of other dogs. They accept their crates as their personal "houses" and seem to be content with their routine and thrive on trying their best to please me.

A Shar-Pei will adjust its lifestyle around your daily schedule, however, it is important to remember that he will need some exercise every day.

SOCIALIZING AND TRAINING

Many prospective puppy buyers lack experience regarding the proper socialization and training needed to develop the type of pet we all desire. In the first 18 months, training does take some work. Trust me, it is easier to start proper training before there is a problem that needs to be corrected.

The initial work begins with the breeder. The breeder should start socializing the puppy at five to six weeks of age and cannot let up. Human socializing is critical up through 12 weeks of age and likewise important during the following months. The litter should be left together during the first few weeks but it is necessary to separate them by ten weeks of age. Leaving them together after that time will increase competition for litter dominance. If puppies are not socialized with people by 12 weeks of age, they will be timid in later life.

The eight- to ten-week age period is a fearful time for puppies. They need to be handled very gently around children and adults. There should be no harsh discipline during this time. Starting at 14 weeks of age, the puppy begins the juvenile period, which ends when he reaches sexual maturity around six to 14 months of age. During the juvenile period he needs to be introduced to strangers (adults, children and other dogs) on the home property. At sexual maturity he will begin to bark at strangers and become more protective. Males start to lift their legs to urinate but if you desire you can inhibit this behavior by walking your boy on leash away from trees, shrubs, fences, etc.

Perhaps you are thinking about an older puppy. You need to inquire about the puppy's social experience. If he has lived in a kennel, he may have a hard time adjusting to people and environmental stimuli. Assuming he has had a good social upbringing, there are advantages to an older puppy.

Separating your Shar-Pei puppy from his littermates to bring him home may be traumatic; however, don't rush the process and he'll adjust in due time.

Puppies who remain with their littermates for eight weeks will have the advantage of good doggie manners and more social disposition.

Training includes puppy kindergarten and a minimum of one to two basic training classes. During these classes you will learn how to dominate your youngster. This is especially important if you own a large breed of dog. It is somewhat harder, if not nearly impossible, for some owners to be the Alpha figure when their dog towers over them. You will be taught how to properly restrain your dog. This concept is important. Again it puts you in the Alpha position. All dogs need to be restrained many times during their lives. Believe it or not, some of our worst offenders are the eight-week-old puppies that are brought to our clinic. They need to be gently restrained for a nail trim but the way they carry on you would think we were killing them. In comparison, their vaccination is a "piece of cake." When we ask dogs to do something that is not agreeable to them, then their worst comes out. Life will be easier for your dog if you expose him at a young age to the necessities of life—proper behavior and restraint.

UNDERSTANDING THE DOG'S LANGUAGE

Most authorities agree that the dog is a descendent of the wolf. The dog and wolf have similar traits. For instance both are pack oriented and prefer not to be isolated for long periods of time. Another characteristic is that the dog, like the wolf, looks to the leader—Alpha—for direction. Both the wolf and the dog communicate through body language, not only within their pack but with outsiders.

Every pack has an Alpha figure. The dog looks to you, or should look to you, to be that leader. If your dog doesn't receive the proper training and guidance, he very well may replace you as Alpha. This would be a serious problem and is certainly a disservice to your dog.

Eye contact is one way the Alpha wolf keeps order within his pack. You are Alpha so you must establish eye contact with your puppy. Obviously your puppy will have to look at you. Practice eye contact even if you need to hold his head for five to ten seconds at a time. You can give him a treat as a reward. Make sure your eye contact is gentle and not threatening. Later, if he has been naughty, it is permissible to give him a long, penetrating look. I caution you there are some older dogs that never learned eye contact as puppies and cannot accept eye contact. You should avoid eye contact with these dogs since they feel threatened and will retaliate as such.

BODY LANGUAGE

The play bow, when the forequarters are down and the hindquarters are elevated, is an invitation to play. Puppies play

fight, which helps them learn the acceptable limits of biting. This is necessary for later in their lives. Nevertheless, an owner

Practice eye contact with your Shar-Pei puppy so that he may establish you as the Alpha of his pack. Make sure your eye contact is confident but not threatening.

The play bow is an invitation that your Shar-Pei puppy wants to play with you. Accept this as his invitation and enjoy his puppy years.

may be falsely reassured by the playful nature of his dog's aggression. Playful aggression toward another dog or human may be an indication of serious aggression in the future. Owners should never play fight or play tug-of-war with any dog that is inclined to be dominant.

Signs of submission are:
1. Avoids eye contact.
2. Active submission—the dog crouches down, ears back and the tail is lowered.
3. Passive submission—the dog rolls on his side with his hindlegs in the air and frequently urinates.

Signs of dominance are:
1. Makes eye contact.
2. Stands with ears up, tail up and the hair raised on his neck.
3. Shows dominance over another dog by standing at right angles over it.

Dominant dogs tend to behave in characteristic ways such as:
1. The dog may be unwilling to move from his place (i.e., reluctant to give up the sofa if the owner wants to sit there).

2. He may not part with toys or objects in his mouth and may show possessiveness with his food bowl.

3. He may not respond quickly to commands.

4. He may be disagreeable for grooming and dislikes to be petted.

Dogs are popular because of their sociable nature. Those that have contact with humans during the first 12 weeks of life regard them as a member of their own species— their pack. All dogs have the potential for both dominant and submissive behavior. Only through experience and training do they learn to whom it is appropriate to show which behavior. Not all dogs are concerned with dominance but owners need to be aware of that potential. It is wise for the owner to establish his dominance early on.

Unwilling to give up the sofa is a sign that your Shar-Pei is expressing his dominance. Proper training tactics must be used to break him of this behavior.

A human can express dominance or submission toward a dog in the following ways:

1. Meeting the dog's gaze signals dominance. Averting the gaze signals submission. If the dog growls or threatens, averting the gaze is the first avoiding action to take—it may prevent attack. It is important to establish eye contact in the puppy. The older dog that has not been exposed to eye contact may see it as a threat and will not be willing to submit.

2. Being taller than the dog signals dominance; being lower signals submission. This is why, when attempting to make friends with a strange dog or catch the runaway, one should kneel down to his level. Some owners see their

dogs become dominant when allowed on the furniture or on the bed. Then he is at the owner's level.

Ultimate submission for a dog is to lie on its back and expose its belly.

3. An owner can gain dominance by ignoring all the dog's social initiatives. The owner pays attention to the dog only when he obeys a command.

No dog should be allowed to achieve dominant status over any adult or child. Ways of preventing are as follows:

1. Handle the puppy gently, especially during the three- to four-month period.
2. Let the children and adults handfeed him and teach him to take food without lunging or grabbing.
3. Do not allow him to chase children or joggers.
4. Do not allow him to jump on people or mount their legs. Even females may be inclined to mount. It is not only a male habit.
5. Do not allow him to growl for any reason.
6. Don't participate in wrestling or tug-of-war games.
7. Don't physically punish puppies for aggressive behavior. Restrain him from repeating the infraction and teach an alternative behavior. Dogs should earn everything they receive from their owners. This would include sitting to receive petting or treats, sitting before going out the door and sitting to receive the collar and leash. These types of exercises reinforce the owner's dominance.

Young children should never be left alone with a dog. It is important that children learn some basic obedience commands so they have some control over the dog. They will gain the respect of their dog.

FEAR

One of the most common problems dogs experience is being fearful. Some dogs are more afraid than others. On the lesser side, which is sometimes humorous to watch, my dog can be afraid of a strange object. He acts silly when something is out of place in the house. I call his problem perceptive intelligence. He realizes the abnormal within his known environment. He does not react the same way in strange environments since he does not know what is normal.

On the more serious side is a fear of people. This can result in backing off, seeking his own space and saying "leave me alone" or it can result in an aggressive behavior that may lead to challenging the person. Respect that the dog wants to be left alone and give him time to come forward. If you approach the cornered dog, he may resort to snapping. If you leave him alone, he may decide to come forward, which should be rewarded with a treat. Years ago we had a dog that behaved in this manner. We coaxed people to stop by the house and make friends with our fearful dog. She learned to take the treats and after weeks of work she overcame her suspicions and made friends more readily.

Have friends and their families stop by to meet your puppy to help accustom him to as many different people as possible.

Some dogs may initially be too fearful to take treats. In these cases it is helpful to make sure the dog hasn't eaten for about 24 hours. Being a little hungry encourages him to accept the treats, especially if

they are of the "gourmet" variety. I have a dog that worries about strangers since people seldom stop by my house. Over the years she has learned a cue and jumps up quickly to visit anyone sitting on the sofa. She learned by herself that all guests on the sofa were to be trusted friends. I think she felt more comfortable with them being at her level, rather than towering over her.

Dogs can be afraid of numerous things, including loud noises and thunderstorms. Invariably the owner rewards (by comforting) the dog when it shows signs of fearfulness. I had a terrible problem with my favorite dog in the Utility obedience class. Not only was he intimidated in the class but he was afraid of noise and afraid of displeasing me. Frequently he would knock down the bar jump, which clattered dreadfully. I gave him credit because he continued to try to clear it, although he was terribly scared. I finally learned to "reward" him every time he knocked down the jump. I would jump up and down, clap my hands and tell him how great he was. My psychology worked, he relaxed and eventually cleared the jump with ease. When your dog is frightened, direct his attention to something else and act happy. Don't dwell on his fright.

AGGRESSION

Some different types of aggression are: predatory, defensive, dominance, possessive, protective, fear induced, noise provoked, "rage" syndrome (unprovoked aggression), maternal and aggression directed toward other dogs. Aggression is the

Puppies follow their noses and each other.

most common behavioral problem encountered. Protective breeds are expected to be more aggressive than others but with the proper upbringing they can make very dependable companions. You need to be able to read your dog.

Many factors contribute to aggression including genetics and environment. An improper environment, which may include the living conditions, lack of social life, excessive punishment, being attacked or frightened by an aggressive dog, etc., can all influence a dog's behavior. Even spoiling him and giving too much praise may be detrimental. Isolation and the lack of human contact or exposure to frequent teasing by children or adults also can ruin a good dog.

Puppies normally play fight with their littermates. They learn the acceptable limits of biting.

Genetics can contribute to an aggressive attitude. If you can meet your puppy's relatives, you may be able to assess their temperaments.

Lack of direction, fear, or confusion lead to aggression in those dogs that are so inclined. Any obedience exercise, even the sit and down, can direct the dog and overcome fear and/or confusion. Every dog should learn these commands as a youngster, and there should be periodic reinforcement.

When a dog is showing signs of aggression, you should speak calmly (no screaming or hysterics) and firmly give a command that he understands, such as the sit. As soon as your dog obeys, you have assumed your dominant position. Aggression presents a problem because there may be danger to others. Sometimes it is an emotional issue. Owners may consciously or unconsciously encourage their dog's aggression. Other owners show responsibility by accepting the problem and taking measures to keep it under control. The owner is responsible for his dog's actions, and it is not wise to take a chance on someone being bitten, especially a child. Euthanasia is the solution for some owners and in severe cases this may be the best choice. However, few dogs are that dangerous and very few are that much of a threat to their owners. If caution is exercised and professional help is gained early on, then I surmise most cases can be controlled.

Some authorities recommend feeding a lower protein (less than 20 percent) diet. They believe this can aid in reducing aggression. If the dog loses weight, then vegetable oil can be added. Veterinarians and behaviorists are having some success with pharmacology. In many cases treatment is possible and

Some authorities believe that a lower protein diet can reduce aggression in dogs. See your veterinarian before you change your Shar-Pei's diet.

can improve the situation.

If you have done everything according to "the book" regarding training and socializing and are still having a behavior problem, don't procrastinate. It is important that the problem gets attention before it is out of hand. It is estimated that 20 percent of a veterinarian's time may be devoted to dealing with problems before they become so intolerable that the dog is separated from its home and owner. If your veterinarian isn't able to help, he should refer you to a behaviorist.

Establish certain rules in the house the very first day you bring your Shar-Pei puppy home. He might be cute on the couch, however, the adult will be difficult to keep off.

PROBLEMS

Barking

This is a habit that shouldn't be encouraged. Over the years I've had new puppy owners call to say that their dog hasn't learned to bark. I assure them they are indeed fortunate but not to worry. Some owners desire their dog to bark so as to be a watchdog. In my experience, most dogs will bark when a stranger comes to the door.

The new puppy frequently barks or whines in the crate in his strange environment and the owner reinforces the puppy's bad behavior by going to him during the night. This is a no-no. I tell my new owners to smack the top of the crate and say "quiet" in a loud, firm voice. The puppies don't like to hear the loud noise of the crate being banged. If the barking is sleep-interrupting, then the owner should take crate and pup to the bedroom for a few days until the puppy becomes adjusted to his new environment. Otherwise ignore the barking during the night.

Barking can be an inherited problem or a bad habit learned through the environment. It takes dedication to stop the barking. Attention should be paid to the cause of the barking.

Does the dog seek attention, does he need to go out, is it feeding time, is it occurring when he is left alone, is it a protective bark, etc.? Presently I have a ten-week-old puppy that is a real loud mouth, which I am sure is an inherited tendency. Both her mother and especially her grandmother are overzealous barkers but fortunately have mellowed with the years. My young puppy is corrected with a firm "no" and gentle shaking and she is responding. When barking presents a problem for you, try to stop it as soon as it begins.

Few of your friends will appreciate having a Shar-Pei jump up on them. Be sure to properly train your dog to keep his paws where they belong.

There are electronic collars available that are supposed to curb barking. Personally I have not had experience with them. There are some disadvantages to to the collar. If the dog is barking out of excitement, punishment is not the appropriate treatment. Presumably there is the chance the collar could be activated by other stimuli and thereby punish the dog when it is not barking. Should you decide to use one, then you should seek help from a person with experience with that type of collar. In my opinion I feel the root of the problem needs to be investigated and corrected.

In extreme circumstances (usually when there is a problem with the neighbors), some people have resorted to having their dogs debarked. I caution you that the dog continues to bark but usually only a squeaking sound is heard. Frequently the vocal cords grow back. Probably the biggest concern is that the dog can be left with scar tissue which can narrow the opening to the trachea.

Jumping Up

Personally, I am not thrilled when other dogs jump on me but I have hurt feelings if they don't! I do encourage my own dogs to jump on me, on command. Some do and some don't. In my opinion, a dog that jumps up is a happy dog. Nevertheless few guests appreciate dogs jumping on them. Clothes get footprinted and/or snagged.

I am a believer in allowing the puppy to jump up during his first few weeks. In my opinion if you correct him too soon and at the wrong age you may intimidate him. Consequently he

could be timid around humans later in his life. However, there will come a time, probably around four months of age, that he needs to know when it is okay to jump and when he is to show off good manners by sitting instead.

Some authorities never allow jumping. If you are irritated by your dog jumping up on you, then you should discourage it from the beginning. A larger breed of dog can cause harm to a senior citizen. Some are quite fragile. It may not take much to cause a topple that could break a hip.

How do you correct the problem? All family members need to participate in teaching the puppy to sit as soon as he starts to jump up. The sit must be practiced every time he starts to jump up. Don't forget to praise him for his good behavior. If an older dog has acquired the habit, grasp his paws and squeeze tightly. Give a firm "No." He'll soon catch on. Remember the entire family must take part. Each time you allow him to jump up you go back a step in training.

Digging

Bored dogs release their frustrations through mischievous behavior such as digging.Dogs shouldn't be left unattended outside, even if they are in a fenced-in yard. Usually the dog is sent to "jail" (the backyard) because the owner can't tolerate him in the house. The culprit feels socially deprived and needs to be included in the owner's life. The owner has neglected the dog's training. The dog has not developed into the companion we desire. If you are one of these owners, then perhaps it is possible for you to change. Give him another chance. Some owners object to their dog's unkempt coat and doggy odor. See that he is groomed on a regular schedule and look into some training classes.

My most important advice to you is to be aware of your dog's actions. Even so, remember dogs are dogs and will behave as such even though we might like them to be perfect little people.When there is reason for concern—don't waste time. Seek guidance. Dogs are meant to be loved and enjoyed.

References:
Manual of Canine Behavior, Valerie O'Farrell, British Small Animal Veterinary Association.
Good Owners, Great Dogs, Brian Kilcommons, Warner Books.

SUGGESTED READING

TS-205
*Successful Dog
Training
160 pages, 130
color photos.*

TS-252
*Dog Behavior
and Training
288 pages,
nearly 200
color photos.*

TS-249
*Skin & Coat Care
for Your Dog
224 pages, 300
color photos.*

TS-214
*Owner's Guide
to Dog Health
432 pages, 300
color photos.*

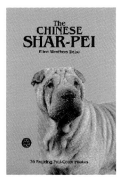

TS-258
*Training Your
Dog for Sports
and Other
Activities
160 pages, over
200 color photos.*

PS-818
*The Chinese
Shar-Pei
256 pages, over
100 full color
photos.*

TS-176
*World of the
Shar-Pei
304 pages,
over 400 full-
color photos.*

TS-150
*Book of the
Shar-Pei
303 pages, over
200 full-color
photos.*

INDEX